The Collected Longer Poems

of Kenneth Rexroth

Books by Kenneth Rexroth

POEMS

Collected Shorter Poems
Collected Longer Poems
New Poems

PLAYS

Beyond the Mountains

EDITOR

Selected Poetry of D. H. Lawrence
New British Poets

TRANSLATIONS

Fourteen Poems of O. V. Lubicz-Milosz
Love and the Turning Year
(*One Hundred More Poems from the Chinese*)
One Hundred Poems from the Chinese
One Hundred Poems from the Japanese
One Hundred More Poems from the Japanese
One Hundred French Poems
One Hundred Poems from the Greek Anthology
Thirty Spanish Poems of Love and Exile
Selected Poems of Pierre Reverdy

ESSAYS

Bird in the Bush
Assays
The Classics Revisited
The Alternative Society

AUTOBIOGRAPHY

An Autobiographical Novel

Kenneth Rexroth

The Collected Longer Poems

New Directions

Copyright 1944, 1950, 1951 by New Directions Publishing Corporation.
Copyright © 1968 by New Directions Publishing Corporation.
Copyright 1952, 1953 by Kenneth Rexroth.
Copyright © 1957, 1967, 1968 by Kenneth Rexroth.

Library of Congress Catalog Card Number: 68-25549
ISBN: 0-8112-0177-5

All rights reserved. Except for brief passages quoted
in a newspaper, magazine, radio, or television review,
no part of this book may be reproduced in any form or
by any means, electronic or mechanical, including
photocopying and recording, or by any information
storage and retrieval system, without permission
in writing from the Publisher.

ACKNOWLEDGMENTS
The first ten sections of "The Heart's Garden, the Garden's Heart"
were first published in book form by the Pym-Randall Press. "The
Homestead Called Damascus" was first published in *The Quarterly
Review of Literature*, Volume IX, Number 2, 1957.

Manufactured in the United States of America

First published clothbound in 1968
First published as New Directions Paperbook 309 in 1970

New Directions Books are published for James Laughlin
by New Directions Publishing Corporation,
333 Sixth Avenue, New York 10014

THIRD PRINTING

Contents

INTRODUCTION TO THE COLLECTED
LONGER POEMS

"The Homestead Called Damascus" was written before I
was twenty years old. The two final pieces, *addenda* to "The
Heart's Garden, The Garden's Heart" were finished after the
book had gone to the publisher. Written between five and
ten years apart, all the sections of this book now seem to me
almost as much one long poem as do *The Cantos* or *Pater-
son*. The plot remains the same—the interior and exterior
adventures of two poles of a personality. The brothers Se-
bastian and Thomas are still, really, arguing with each other
right to the last page, and the third figure—the anonymous
observer—is still making wry comments. Partly, each of the
separate long poems is a philosophical revery—but a revery
in dialogue in which philosophies come and go. The sections
in "The Phoenix and the Tortoise" and "The Dragon and
the Unicorn" which expound a systematic view of life are
dramatic dialogue, not the sole exposition of the author, and
always they are contradicted by the spokesman for the other
member of the polarity. If there is any dialectic resolution, it
occurs each time in the unqualified, transcendent experience
which usually ends each long poem. The ending of "A Pro-
legomenon to a Theodicy" may be more conventionally
mystical, but after this the lesson has been learned, the ladder
has been climbed, and so is kicked away. The recurring word
is, "visions are a measure of the defect of vision."

In my *Collected Shorter Poems* are some that are long but
not "longer" which well could go in temporal sequence with
those in this book. "The Thin Edge of Your Pride," the story
"When You Asked for It Did You Get It," "Organon," "Ice
Shall Cover Nineveh," and even "Past and Future Turn
About," a pendant to "The Phoenix and the Tortoise," just
as sections of the long poems, especially of "The Dragon
and the Unicorn," stand as "shorter poems" in their own

right. Most poets resemble Whitman in one regard—they write only one book and that an interior autobiography.

Besides the triad of witnesses, there are other members of the cast, other *personae* of the person. Most important, of course, are the girls and women who come and go, the polarity to which the dialectic of the Twins and their commentator together form a pole. From Leda's eggs sprang not only Castor and Pollux, divine and human, but Helen and Clytemnestra, innocence and power. Marichi, an avatar of the Shakti of Shiva, has three heads: a sow, a woman in orgasm and the Dawn. "Goddess of the Dawn," as Westerners call her, her chariot drawn by swine, she haunts "The Homestead Called Damascus" and comes back as a beautiful Communist girl in "The Heart's Garden"—as does Vega, the jewel in the Lyre, the Weaving Girl who weaves and ravels and weaves again.

Sebastian returns in another martyrdom in "Thou Shalt Not Kill." And in the verse plays, *Beyond the Mountains* [now published by City Lights Books], the same cast of characters deals even more explicitly with the same themes. In the plays the women take over the consequences of the men in the longer poems as the descendants of Genji's friend Tojo no Chujo take over the Bodhisattva perfume from Genji. Who stands for who? The vicarity is ambivalent. Who blinds who on the road to Damascus with all-illuminating light? *Lux lucis et fons luminis*—the threads are still weaving in Kyoto, Mount Calvary above Santa Barbara in California, at the Cowley Fathers by the Charles and on the loom set up across the Hudson at Holy Cross in the opening of "The Homestead."

The political stance of the poems never changes—the only Absolute is the Community of Love with which Time ends. Time is the nisus toward the Community of Love. One passage is a statement in philosophical terms of the I.W.W. Preamble, another of the cash nexus passage in *The Communist Manifesto*. "The State is the organization of the evil instincts of mankind." "Liberty is the mother, not the daughter, of order." "Property is robbery." And similar quotations from Tertullian, St. Clement, Origen, St. Augustine.

It is easy to overcome alienation—the net of the cash nexus can simply be stepped out of, but only by the self actualizing man. But everyone is self actualizing and can realize it by the simplest act—the self unselfing itself, the only act that is actual act. I have tried to embody in verse the belief that the only valid conservation of value lies in the assumption of unlimited liability, the supernatural identification of the self with the tragic unity of creative process. I hope I have made it clear that the self does not do this by an act of will, by sheer assertion. He who would save his life must lose it.

"What endures, what perishes?" The permanent core of thought could perhaps be called a kind of transcendental empiricism—"the 'ineluctable modality' of the invisible." The real objects are their own transcendental meaning. If reality can be apprehended without grasping, the epistemological problem vanishes. The beginning of experience is the same as the end of it. The source or spring of knowing is the same as the fulfillment of it—experience begins and ends in il-lumination. The holy is in the heap of dust—it is the heap of dust. Beyond the object lies a person—objects are only perspectives on persons. But the experience of either is ulti-mately unqualifiable. Epistemology is moral. There is no "problem." Visions are problems. Vision is the solution that precedes the problem. It is precisely the thing in itself that we do experience. The rest is reification. So too the I-Thou relationship is primary. The dialogue comes after. Everything else is manipulation—reification again—and so, illusion. It is love and love alone . . . as it says in the old popular song.

"Thus literally living in a blaze of glory." True illumina-tion is habitude. We are unaware that we live in the light of lights because it casts no shadow. When we become aware of it we know it as birds know air and fish know water. It is the ultimate trust.

"If thee does not turn to the Inner Light, where will thee turn?"

Kenneth Rexroth

Whitsunday, 1968

THE HOMESTEAD CALLED
DAMASCUS
(1920–1925)

For
Leslie
Dorothy

THE HOMESTEAD CALLED DAMASCUS

I

Heaven is full of definite stars
And crowded with modest angels, robed
In tubular, neuter folds of pink and blue.
Their feet tread doubtless on that utter
Hollowness, with never a question
Of the "ineluctable modality"
Of the invisible; busy, orderly,
Content to ignore the coal pockets
In the galaxy, dark nebulae,
And black broken windows into space.
Youthful minds may fret infinity,
Moistly dishevelled, poking in odd
Corners for unsampled vocations
Of the spirit, while the flesh is strong.
Experience sinks its roots in space—
Euclidean, warped, or otherwise.
The will constructs rhomboids, nonagons,
And paragons in time to suit each taste.
Or, if not the will, then circumstance.
History demands satisfaction,
And never lacks, with or without help
From the subjects of its curious science.

Thomas Damascan and the mansion,
A rambling house with Doric columns
On the upper Hudson in the Catskills,
Called Damascus. We were walking there
Once in early Spring; his brother Sebastian
Said, staring into the underbrush,
"If you'll look close you'll see the panthers
In there eating the crocus." And Thomas said,
"Panthers are always getting into
The crocus. Every spring. There were too many

3

Panthers about the courts in my father's time."
They had an odd wry sort of family humor
That startled idle minds and plagued your
Memory for years afterwards.
We sat up late that night drinking wine,
Playing chess, arguing—Plato and Leibnitz,
Einstein, Freud and Marx, and woke at noon.
The next day was grey and rained till twilight,
And ice from somewhere in the Adirondacks
Drifted soggily down the river.
In the afternoon Sebastian read
The Golden Bough, and Thomas said,
"Remember, in school, after we read Frazer,
I insisted on signing myself Tammuz,
To the horror of all our teachers?"
"And now," he said, "We're middle aged, wise,"
(They were very far from middle aged.)
"And what we thought once was irony
Is simple fact, simple, sensuous,
And so forth. Fate is a poor scholar."
We said nothing, and the three of us
Watched the rain fall through the budding trees,
Until at last Thomas rose and took
A bow from the rack, sprung it, and said,
"I wish we could shoot these things in the rain."
Sebastian said, "I'd much rather shoot
In the sunshine, and besides it spoils
The arrows. I'm going for a hike."
So we went off through the hanging woods,
Single file, and up the steep meadow,
Scratched by thistles, in a thistle wind—
Last year's thistles, and a pungent wind.
Thomas said, "We've got to move the goats
Before they ruin all the pasture.
There'll be nothing but thistles next year."
Sebastian said, "Thistles or blue grass,
Goats or cattle, what does it matter,
We'll have to die quick to be buried here."
The goats hurried ahead up the slope,
Stopped among the rocks and there gave us

4

Their clinical goatish regard.
We climbed to the top of the Pope's Nose
And stood looking out at the river,
Slaty in the rain, and the traffic
Wallowing on the muddy highway,
And beneath us in the closed hollow,
The swollen carp ponds, the black water
Flowing through the clattering rushes,
And, poised each on one cold leg, two herons,
Staring over their puckered shoulders
At a hieroglyph of crows in the distance.

"Leslie wants to see us," Thomas said.
"I think they are giving a party."
In the evening, after dinner, we
Took the canoe across the river,
Drifting downstream in the blue twilight.
Another columned house but with great
Windows full of the darkening sky.
Some people in bare shoulders and white shirt fronts
Were standing about in candlelight,
Listening to Leslie play the clavichord.
She looked very precious and British
In her thick braids and bronze green velvet.
While she sang Lawes' *Go Lovely Rose*,
Sebastian watched an Autumn moth flown
Delicately from the garden to
Rest in pale sienna on his hand.
He saw her with her father's falcons,
Greensleeves and moth breasted birds and pale
Braided hair, riding side saddle, dressed
In velvet. Daytimes she wore a chatelaine,
And this in twentieth century,
Upstate New York—Guardi and Longhi
On the walls. The moth, he noticed, had
Green eyes, a Horus head, antennae
Thrown over its wings like plumed eyebrows.
It titivated much like a fly.
Somebody had a flute—they were playing
Debussy's trio now—music for the moth.

There were two moths now, one rushing through
The candelabrum on the clavichord;
And from his hand the green eyed Horus
Lifted and took his undulant way
Towards the music, across the peopled room.

Sebastian stood alone in the hollow dark
And watched the long lift of resounding
Black water, the march and counter march
Of the white wave crests. Alone in the spray
Filled rushing night he walked the shingle
Barefoot, with wet open lips, his nostrils
Flaring to the beating air. There were
Figures in the night, unseen but there,
Invisible journeys begun and
Ended there at the land's end amongst
The damp odorous sea litter.
Springing from such a shingle over
Such water went the perilous bridge
To the shining city, went the knight
Who did not come back and the red
Single star. Sebastian tires and turns,
Back to the sleeping village, back to
The dim lit station, the late slow train,
And the city of steel and concrete towers.
He will know many days of walks in
Little parks of dead leaves and sparrows,
Afternoon with fountains in the haze,
And the martyrdom of arrows.

The sheep are passing in the snow,
Their hooves aclatter on the frozen marsh.
Before them and behind them go
The wading shepherds, tall and bent.
And Thomas, with a narrow light,
Comes out and watches, by the gate;
And muses in the turgid night;
And goes into the house again.
The library is calm and prim.

The shepherds and the sheep have passed.
And Botticelli ladies, slim
And hyperthyroid, grace the walls.

The rose astonished Sebastian and
He was astonished that some day he
Would be irretrievably quite dead.
Beside the rose he placed a small worn
Stone that had been loved and tended by
Some undersea Brancusi. He thought
Of the electron and the nebula.
His mind was like a dark vault full of
Spider webs of light. He thought of Spring
And Thomas long ago expounding
The *Timaeus* in the rainy night—
Damascus in bygone Spring weather.
Now he pressed his thumb against the stone
And watched and waited expectantly.
Once he watched the hopeful young poplar
Day by day shivering up towards
Heaven. It seemed almost transparent
In the level afternoon sunlight
With here and there its artificial
Leaves pinned on like fine ground scales of jade.
Years before he had written a poem—
"Between slender trees a drowse of petals falls."

Suddenly he came on the footprint
Of a Picasso nude on the dull
Red sand beneath the grey heat of skies
Of some very different chemistry.
Her lips moved exactly as always,
Saying the same irrevocable,
Common things. Outside, winter evening
Lay blue and electric on the snow.
And in the room the asbestos glow
Came from the gas log efficiently.
He thought of all the things that had been
Fossilized safely so long ago.
He could not forget in César Franck

Or Haydn or the evening paper.
Somewhere there was still an old dry world
Of trouble and amazement filled with
Things of stone and meditation. Then,
Too, there was a humid garden where
In the lewd green dark a lewd white
Animal minced kneelessly away.
Somewhere far off the rigid granite
Flames revolved across the steppe and high eyes
Swung to the right and left horizon.

Sebastian dreamed and saw the room, marked
With the dwelling of her ordered hands,
Saw her favorite poems turned down
On the sewing table, and shadows
Curled like tabby cats around the pots,
Saw the chairs arranged as she liked them,
The broken chaise longue by the orchard
Window where the morning sun came in,
The same atmosphere of bosom calm.
Her fingers had just run through his hair.
He dreamed, "She is in another room
Or out shopping. She will be back soon."
And then into his sleep from waking
Hours came the memory that things
Had not been this way for many years.
Dreaming, Sebastian said, "That was a dream."
And slowly he awoke and said, half
Dreaming, "Bishop Berkeley's cherries are
Still weighted with me. I shall sit for
Many a day eating illusions,
And dream at night and in the morning
Wake to the same worn out cruelty."

Sebastian said, "There is a coral
Garden path which ends at a statue
Of Priapus. In my mind a man
And woman walk along it and do
Not come back. The ooze of the sea floor
Red with rust of countless meteors

Covers the broken gold forgotten
There. I know a diver once went mad,
He said he'd seen Atlantis, the rooms
Of the courtesans bright with electric
Fish and octopus hanging from the
Ceilings of the temples. When I left
He said, 'I have seen that poor city.' "
Sebastian, sitting in Romany
Marie's one stormy evening, watching
The green distorted faces pass the
Street lamp, watching the distorted
Silhouettes on the drawn shades of the
Tenement across the street, listens
To gitanas on the phonograph
And drinks a glass of fermented milk.

Thomas remembered the panthers' soft
Cries, mating once in the underbrush,
As he climbed alone through the rafters,
Past the sleeping bells and bats and owls.
Here the devil came to play cribbage
With the sexton, here the prayers go past
On small bright tinkling metallic wings,
The ghosts of votive lamps in their beaks.
This dusky ascension is peopled
With more than horned and hairy shadows.
Here is the long comrade, the little
Brother of death with his chalk old skull,
This is the other with his mincing
Fellowship, and here is the man with
The vorpal blade, who is pale because of the
Surrounding darkness. Alone
In this prehistoric night, each naked
Marionette is dismayed at his
Own conduct and flees, leaving a spoor
Of scratches on the snow. Before this
He had remembered the brown darkness,
The trigonometry of the rafters,
The astronomy of the ladders,
Long before this, alone among the panthers.

Modred observed the static terror
Of the poised archaic archangels.
Lucifer gave fire, guided the Kabbala
To chemistry and back again. Death
Where hinges fall, a land of crusts and
Rusted keys, the desert colored like
A lumpy fog, geologic ages
Of searing suns—consider that place.
Modred, the dark and crimson man, rose
And walked from the place called the skull, walked
Far, and the Lamb beside him like a
Star, with feet of stars and flowers walked.
Dark Modred covertly from his bloody eyes
Beyond the tangled thicket and the thorns saw
Hakeldama, the potter's field
Full of dead strangers.

II

THE AUTUMN OF MANY YEARS

In a ruddy light, in a craggy
Land, where at the turning of the paths,
Horrible stone figures slipped away
As they approached, Thomas descended
Slowly towards the empty city from which
Alternate noise and utter stillness
Came. Sebastian halted, waited at
The last hill crest and watched him go.
Beyond the place he stopped not a leaf
Or blade of grass appeared nor any
Warm or cold blooded moving thing. He
Waited. The dogs nuzzled his knees, and
Whined. It grew dark. He waited all night.

Forgotten, unknown, anonymous,
He threads his way through narrow places

Between the worn hills. He is alone
Where there are dim forms, fronds of sorrow
Spreading in the close dusk of rock and
Horizontal pines. His face is pale
In the dimness, and his pale hands part
The ever present leafy curtain,
Gently, wisely, as if he parted
The green velvet bodice and skirt
Of a weak girl. The green dimness grows.
He vanishes in the vegetable light.

"This is my scene, this part must I
Fulfill." So life turns back upon
Itself. Sebastian at last came to
An afternoon, a parcel of hours
In the Autumn of many years.
A time which he had always known,
A passing light in which he had
Always lived. A heart beat in the clock.
Stars, blue flowers and blue unicorns?
Perhaps Thomas's rutting panthers?
His own especial arc in time curved
And then went flat around him, moment
And century in which he lived life—
This bland forever, known forever,
An Autumn afternoon, Damascus
With the brown rock lunging from the elm,
The oak leaf scuff in the level light.

Webster one morning after breakfast
Knew, "Like diamonds we are cut with our
Own dust." Sebastian sat in the
Broken belvedere above the river
Playing chess with himself and drinking
Not wine, nor whiskey, but bitter tea,
Cold and steeped too long. The two knights moved
Reciprocally. One side was sure
To lose. Relatives came to visit
The instant. Every instant has them.

11

Sebastian thought, "I have no relatives.
I am like the little figure of
Daruma secreted in the last
Encapsuled Japanese box. I am
All alone at Christmas time somewhere
Like Durban, Bergen, or Singapore."
He unfolded the revolving knights.
The pattern seemed to be different now.
Sebastian finished the astringent tea.
"Like myself," he said, "This is getting
Nowhere," and went back to the house and
To a book he had turned down.

In the deep blue winter evening
The homeward crowd murmurs and hurries
And rearranges itself to the
Color of signal lights and shrilling
Whistles. Sebastian disengages
Himself and walks in the cold, smoky
Twilight of Central Park, spotted with
Week old dirty snow, and stands to watch
The skaters, skating there beneath the
Acrid revelation of forty
Floodlights. Northward many nightbound miles
Gathering the winter about it
Damascus keeps the long January
Darkness. Once in a long while, far off,
Men move, very small with very small
Bright lanterns, and the frosted breath of
Old dogs clouds their footsteps as they fall.
Foxes on the mountain go delicate
Across the snow on sly fox errands.

Something living passed this way, something
Alive and dreamed about. The steep bulge
Of the pale expansive hills arches
Gently over that other world. The moon
Is transparent as a soap bubble
And looks as likely to burst. Somewhere
A violin awakes and says, "A blonde."

The uneasy souls of men arrange
Themselves on streetcar platforms. Autumn.
Thought wanders like goose crossed smoke. And all
The stone and ironic city turns
To smoke and glass, to verticals of
Rose and lavender. And then there comes
The blue and saffron moment, nighthawks
Cry and plunge above the roofs, and waste
Paper settles in the dirty courtyards,
And pigeons murmur and settle in
The cornices. Burnt fried potatoes,
Automobile smoke and one lonely
Rattling streetcar. Something living passed—
Invisible in the haze, but alive.

Haitian drums or African and horns
From New Orleans. She rolls her buttocks
Like kelp on the sea surge or taffy
In a churn. Rhinestones cover her bee-stung
Pussy and perch on each nipple. Drums
Roll as she rolls her belly and her eyes.
Grove or colonnade, porch or garden—
White, blue and silver garments and long
Carefully tended beards and hands.
Sebastian paints a Rousseau landscape
Of gnarled pine and giant dogwood, paths
Of pink coral and stone moon bridges
Over obese gold fish. "Figures by
Another hand." The School of Athens?
He waits for her act to end. She smiles
A warm domestic smile. The band explodes.
The rhinestones fall. A polar wind blows
Down South State Street under the Northern
Lights. The taxi bores into the Rousseau
Landscape of warm domesticity.
The figures are by another hand.

The Lotophagi with their silly hands
Haunt me in sleep, plucking at my sleeve;
Their gibbering laughter and blank eyes

Hide on the edge of the mind's vision
In dusty subways and crowded streets.
Late in August, asleep, Adonis
Appeared to me, frenzied and bleeding
And showed me, clutched in his hand, the plow
That broke the dream of Persephone.
The next day, regarding the scorched grass
In the wilting park, I became aware
That beneath me, beneath the gravel
And the hurrying ants, and the loam
And the subsoil, lay the glacial drift,
The Miocene jungles, the reptiles
Of the Jurassic, the cuttlefish
Of the Devonian, Cambrian
Worms, and the mysteries of the gneiss;
Their histories folded, docketed
In darkness; and deeper still the hot
Black core of iron, and once again
The inscrutable archaic rocks,
And the long geologic ladder,
And the living soil and the strange trees,
And the tangled bodies of lovers
Under the strange stars.
                              And beside me,
A mad old man, plucking at my sleeve.

Persephone awaits him in the dim boudoir,
Waits him, for the hour is at hand.
She has arranged the things he likes
Near to his expected hand:
Herrick's poems, tobacco, the juice
Of pomegranates in a twisted glass.
She piles her drugged blonde hair
Above her candid forehead,
Touches up lips and eyelashes,
Selects her most naked robe.
On the stroke of the equinox he comes,
And smiles, and stretches his arms, and strokes
Her cheeks and childish shoulders, and kisses
The violet lids closed on the grey eyes.

14

Free of aggressive Aphrodite,
Free of the patronizing gods,
The cruel climate of Olympus,
They feed caramels to Cerberus
And warn him not to tell
The cuckold Pluto of their adulteries,
Their mortal lechery in dispassionate Hell.

Nobody knows him, nobody cares.
He is alone in a foreign place.
He cannot understand their ways. He
Cannot appreciate the beauty
Of the landscape. "Here are his footprints,"
They say, "He went this way, through the woods,
Over the rocks and towards the desert."
They say, "There was nobody with him."
He and she, matching stride for stride, pace
The garden walks. It was very
Pleasant where they went. He chews his sun
Baked mustache. Her eyes are almost closed.
They say, "See, these are his footprints, still
Black in the early morning hoarfrost."

You can see through the level days
A long way, clear to the end of life,
Through the bars of pale gold level sunlight.
In the evening the blunt fingers
Of shadows stammer behind us,
Shadow forests, beams of chaos, collapse
Against the walls, gold and scarlet fire
Cities with avenues of copper
Explode at our feet in crashing earthquakes.
The lamp burns out. Outside in the cold,
Loneliness comes down from between
The far off mountains, like a black fog
Over the prairie. Fire and darkness
After the arid day, arms entwined,
We remember the confused racket
Of rapid water broken by stones.
Afloat again, the green canoe creeps

Slowly down the twisting green water.
Here there are miles of burnished barley,
Pine on the foothills, and the bare red
Ranges streaked with snow. How long ago
We fished in a narrow full river,
In a forest of damp broad leaves.

How short a time for a life to last.
So few years, so narrow a space, so
Slight a melody, a handful of
Notes. Most of it dreams and dreamless sleep,
And solitary walks in empty
Parks and foggy streets. Or all alone,
In the midst of nightstruck, excited
Crowds. Once in a while one of them
Spoke, or a face smiled, but not often.
One or two could recall the tune if asked.
Now she is gone. Hooded candles in
The Spring wind tilt and move down the
Narrow columned aisle. Incense plumes whirl.
Thuribles clink. The last smoke dissolves
Above the rain soaked hills, the black pines,
Broken by a flock of migrating birds.

Thomas climbed the ice and crossed the pass.
Coneys whistled in the shrill air. Ice
And rock and indigo sky—Enoch
Walked the hills and waged war on substance
In the vertical. Is it best to
Remember always the same memory,
To see the world always in the same hour?
Good Friday, incense and hooded candles.
Sebastian descends the wet hillside
Into the coiling river fog. He
Sinks from sight into the hidden world.
And on the mountain crest the tattered
Crows wheel like an apparition
In a fog as serpentine and cold,
And much more opaque, and unseen caw

16

And caw. This hour the sacramental
Man was broken on the height, in dark
Opacity rent with caw and caw.

Thomas, called Tammuz, the first
Of twins, "the beloved one," the one
Called Didymus in the upper room—
The involuntary active man—
Peers in the black wounds, hammers the frame
That squeezes the will. The arrow breaks.
He breaks the gold arrow in the gold
Light. The arrow breaks the brittle flesh,
Breaking upon it. Baldur in the
Autumn, the image of the twin.
The Autumn light, the level lawn.
Modred, Iscariot, Loki cross
Beyond the Catskills. Sebastian drinks
Cold astringent tea in the damp
Summer house above the hazy river.

III

THE DOUBLE HELLAS

Claret enim claris quod clare concopulator

Before the ice the convulsions of
Thought sprawled baroque in baroque forests
Glutted with boa constrictor swamps,
Where green terror stalked the aborigine.
From the mountains where the ice lay waiting
The foggy sun fondled a landscape
Voluptuous and odorous as
Flesh and ambergris. Now high above
Mammoth and behemoth buried in
Immemorial ice the black starved
Procession winds to the tolling of
Black bells. The frozen saint is buried

In a shrill vault of glittering ice.
When the hills appeared again, soggy
And white, only the memories of
Being crept across their faces, only
The creeping shadows of life in the
Long red night beneath the dying sun.

A dry static tightness of pigment,
Aloofness to more accessible
Experience, the hand dry and white
In bygone porcelain drawing rooms,
Hot, dry, indoor wintry afternoons,
Crisp crinolines and bright figures of
Twisted glass. The children coming home
Through the grey green fog that prowled between
The grey stone and dark brick closed house fronts.
And later, the deep blue evenings,
The yellow lights, the humming tile stove,
Father with his silver flute,
Mother singing to the harmonium.
Thomas thought—My parents had that life,
And they in turn recognized themselves
In Henry James and would in Proust
If they had lived long enough, and now
We seem to be unable to escape
From our own ornate, wasted fictions.

There are cannas now on the guarded
Lawns, crimson and Chinese orange, with wine
Brown leaves. The privet hedges are black,
And grey with dust. The thick blood squeezes
In and out of the heart and falls like
Quicksilver down the arteries. The brain
Unrolls in its own vaults its own arid,
Endless frieze. Sebastian strolls along
The narrow privet lanes of the garden
Labyrinth. Ignorant, invisible,
The catechumens move along the wall.
Sebastian idles in the infant
Canyon of small leaves stiff with Autumn.

Floral vulvas of orange and crimson
Squirm inside his head, his fingers snap
The brittle privet leaves. The day sleeps.

The capon sits spatulate, Origen
Among the teacups, the lowering,
Not quite invisible genius of
The case at hand. Manipulations,
Especially ante-Steinach and
Unsure, do not suffice to still the Pauline,
Age-long battle. A puzzled fire
Still hovers. Tin plated words unfold
From her lips, glitter briefly before
Her scarcely moving, maidenly mouth—
Kore entertaining impotent
Hades. Her hands are never still, never
Hurried. The sun declines, the garden
Gives off its perfumes. The conversation
Builds bridges and arches to nowhere.
Cups and wafers move. The fallen flowers
Of the trumpet vine lie like red meat
Underfoot. The dusty hollyhocks
Defend the wall. Last night someone
Kissed her on the moonlit doorstep.
The phallic vermilion flowers rot.
His hands, like huge white grubs, hang dying
To his wrists. Hers build another bridge
And send a covey of words out on it.
The mellow mountains undulate
Down to the river through the blue haze.
The air smoulders with the beginning
Of Autumn. In the background vacant
Figures outlined with thin strokes of white
Move transparently across the landscape.

That was a strange game of chess she played
In Uxmal—a long time ago.
Her fingers move out from her body
And dissolve like faint wisps of gaseous
Gold. Her head jerks, the black lacquered eyes

Stay still. An impenetrable black
Surface falls from them, between her and
The musicians. The music is lost
In an illimitable nightbound
Valley. Her flesh unbraids itself like
A rope. The metal melts and flows away.
Brown, brown, brown is the color of my
True love's skin. Her lips are sweeter than
The full blown rose. Her eyes are sad where
Love has entered in. Graceful and wise
Before my eyes she goes. Her learned
Body and her childish ways possess
All my mind and all my days . . . Maxine. . . .
Uxmal, Konarak, or Ajanta.
His walls have fallen, his painted
Beauties are yellow dust forever now.

The world is composed of a pair of
Broken pillars, a round sun in a
Rigid sky, a sea, and in the great
Distance, a red line of cliffs. The world
Is composed of a pair of broken
Pillars, of pillars, of a suave line
Conceived in a mind infinitely
Refined by edges infinitely
Sharp. The world is composed. There is a
Little boat upon the sea, a striped
Sail. They raise a net from the bright sea
And go away rowing with the wind.
Recently awe and precision hung
In this landscape, the keen edge of pride,
The suave line, the Doric mind. Voices
Of children come up the steep valley.
A blur of smoke smudges the skyline.
"Come back, baby, I miss your little
Brown body and your childish ways."
"Hush, Chloris, heed not the stars
Narcissistically parading
There above the mannered pools."
You can always find pity

And terror amongst the broken
Statuary. Whose profiles
Coin the wind? The Bactrian
Kings. Pisanello's courtesans.
The whole sky is made of gold.
The dancing master in a
Castled wig, Priapus in
The vines. The soft sliding eyes.
"Ah, Chloris, heed not the stars,
The smoky shattering fountains
In the teeming night."

My parents had their life, it was not
Your soft dark tragedy. It was not
Anything like it. Saffron twilights
Over the gas lit horse drawn city.
Purple and gold above the desert.
When they were sad, they shut their mouths tight.
When God spoke to Job from the whirlwind
He refused to answer his questions—
On the advice of his attorney.
The rainbow mountains glitter in
The breaking prism. Within the mirror
Of ice, pain speaks to sorrow outside.
And now the sun has set and the strange
Blake-like forms fade from our memories.
The sky was deeper than a ruby.
The hoarfrost spreads over the marshes
Like a mandolin note over water.
Between the mountains a candle burned.
A narrow leaf of flame casting no
Light about it. The epic hero
Came, in full armor, making a huge
Clatter, and fell, struck down from behind,
And lay in the barren eternal
Dawn, geometrically prostrate,
As the clock ticks measured out his death—
As the spouting flame leaped from roof to
Roof and all the houses full of ticking
Clocks caught fire one after another.

Not rock, not mountains, not twisted pine,
No scar of twisted fire, but water,
The dominion of water, the sound
Of light wind and water in a place
Of watery light. In the turmoil
Of market place or war, in the
Stress of love or music, this place
Will tabernacle the heart. This place
Will be inviolate, the mind's home.
Luminous apple leaves animated
Into a soft glitter of sound. The
Voice of speaking leaves and lustral water.
Hands that moved like soft grave birds,
Tending the flowers in the garden
At Crotona, soft grave eyes and large
Soft grave lips that hardly ever spoke.
She was a street walker, just brought out,
Twelve years old with naked breasts and gauze
Thighs, cuddled in the shadow of the
Golden man headed bull at the gate
Of the Great King. His Greek companions
Said, "There is the goddess, not yet awake."
The Indians called her Marichi,
The Chinese were polite but afraid.
In less than a year, she spoke their language.
They sat before the mountain cottage
High above the great plain of China.
The philosophers, so polite, came
And offered their polite discourses.
She interpreted as best she could.
They lowered their eyes so politely.
His eyes were lambent, like a beast's eyes.
So many long years, usually
The avatars of the goddess are
Short lived. He said, "She had four lives to live.
Love, and wisdom, and sorrow, and joy—
Four fleshly emanations in one flesh."
Aristotle never heard of her.
Iamblichus knew she must have been and
Reinvented her. He called her Theano.

They have put a bust of Bach in the
Little park. Around him they have planted
The old time flowers small town grandmas
Still grow somewhere. Two nuns walk the new
White gravel path, spacing their rosaries
Between a Naiad fountain and the
Bust of Bach. Sebastian is alone.
She is asleep in her scented bed,
The shades drawn, the room warm and dark, her
Body dark and coiled in heavy sleep.
Sebastian reads Socrates on love.
"Putte him bye—." The current flows the other
Way. Or at the most oscillates like
The nuns and their tinkling rosaries.
Her sex sleeps like a dark wet mystic eye.

Sebastian said, "Is this my very creed?
Shall I embody the svelte engines
Of the present fact? Shall personal
Loneliness give way to the enduring
Geological isolation?
Shall the filaments strung to gusty
Brown Autumn roads snap? The tender
Trickles in the Spring woods dry quite up?
Somewhere quests a strange simplicity.
And oh, my music, when she walks
In beauty, through smoking traffic
Between the twilight skyscrapers
The verve undulance of the lonely
Heart. Are you my Narcissus pool?
Brilliant rockets of the sun dappled
Waterfall? Young and beautiful with
Old eyes and quick feet. Philosopher—
No hunk of this matter will receive
Any impression of the pure Idea."

"The book turned down." They left the long halls.
Death came in uncountable fashions.
Death when they passed beneath Caesar's yoke.
The clank and clang of swords and armor.

23

Beatrice, the aeon Beatrice.
The courtesan of the fiery stars.
The old town in mist and falling leaves.
How can you bear to watch me weeping?
How indeed? I wonder at myself.
The stairs collapse, the long halls fall down.
"If I live forever, I shall not
Forget that summer. He and I sat
Late in the hot August evenings
And talked endlessly of the panic
And of our hopes and fears and of my
Historical and economic
Theories, and so the summer wore
Away amidst an excitement verging
On a revolution." Death in Venice?

Thomas said, "This land is too well manured.
In fact it's nothing but dead flesh and rock.
The Thanksgiving turkey bones alone
Make an immense midden. The bedrooms
Mold with the sweat of bygone death beds.
The parlor is choked with meaningless
Bric a brac, the flotsam of India,
The China trade, and whaling round the poles.
And the bark cloth my great grandfather
Wore the night he bedded the princess."
Under the church is a crypt. There are
Bones there, but of a pterodactyl,
Not a man, and beneath the black crypt
A blacker catacomb, ceiling and walls
Painted with women copulating
With beasts and monsters. Before we cleaned them
They could not be seen for the smoke of
The countless torches of underground
Assignations. Thomas said, "She's nice.
But the chirr of bracelets on her wrists,
The scorching hallucination of
Her thighs, her buttocks rolling like two
Struggling slugs—these things are not for me.
I hear them echoing in the tunneled

Sepulcher, once more the underground
Hocus pocus of torches and cavern trysts.
Once more Aholah, and Aholibah.
My arteries and veins are my own.
Pass me the paper." A man alone
In a hazy autumnal garden,
A man alone in a hazy desert.
A man and a woman alone in bed.
Many dead men and women each alone.

I know this is an ambivalent
Vicarity—who stands for who?
And this is the reality, then—
This flesh, the flesh of this arm and I
Know how this flesh lies on this bone
Of this arm, this is reality—
I know. I ask nothing more of it.
These things are beautiful, these are
My sacraments and I ask no more.
Did I dream about the same woman?
My fingers twine on themselves and twine
On the memory of a hand, long
After that hand. My being is her
Dream, she has dreamed that journey and dreamed
That cruel map, that strong manual
Of demands. I know I am her dream.
Now the new brick warehouse shouldering
Strong by the shore of the lake through soft
Smoke, rests in the sunset like the vast
Cheek of a peasant resting on the vast
Chest of her lover. Pied cattle come
Home down hills of young grass once more
In the beautiful hour. Once more
The bridges lift in the blue twilight.
White boats go out. I forgot this is
Undeniably reality.

I had forgotten. The movement of
The lotus horned barge is the symbol
And enunciation of the movement

Of the malachite water and the
Movement of the quartz and the silver
Veinings of fishes, of the golden
Poinsettias of fishes breaking
Before the prow. Behind and below
The lotus horn and the oiled ocher
Of the girls' bare breasts and shoulders,
The young favorite of Ikhnaton
Reclines on a bed of rushes. In
The next picture he stands with wide arms.
His eagerness communicates to
And swells in the flying curve of death,
The throw stick. The pattern breaks into
Breaking birds, rises and shatters in
An interrupted arrow of herons.
In the hands of the girls javelins
Lie long and still. The nervous profile
Of the boy is a perfect example
Of the Tel-el-Amarna decadence.

On the sidewalk the shadows lie sharp
And inviolate in the lonely
Light of a Sunday, unblurred
By smoke in the sharper air. Figures
Paired upon the street—colored and black,
Lean feet to feet like folded fingers.
Heel taps are audible as at night.
Gold, scarlet, mitered, the Cardinal
Fluctuates across the steps between
Furry prisms of incense filled sunlight
And sings the Ite Missa Est closing
The Mystery of the Holy Ghost.
Parmenides was sure he had fixed
The eye fast to vision forever—
The duplication of the crystal cube.
Heraclitus said the world was made
Of the quick red tongue between her lips,
Or else from the honey that welled up
From the shady spring between her thighs.
At Oxford in the dreamy Autumn,

Charles Stuart, King and Martyr to be,
Often known as Shorty to his friends,
Raised his hand and bade the tide to stop.
Let the world stay frozen in a bird's eye—
Let the oak leaf freeze in the mid quiver
At Dodona, let the knife freeze fast
Above Iphigenia's red heart.
Let the long ships wait, let the thought wait,
Let the fleshy flame lick the crystal.

Like doors his thoughts snap shut one after
One with his steps. The tree, moon isolate
In moonless night, stiffens in an
Explosion of wind and rips off every
Leaf. The sky cuts like a cleaver at
His toes. He waits on phosphorescent
Ruts. The way is closed. There was a word.
Once there was some one sure Sesame.
In an immense twilit library
Book after book congeals beneath
The hands. The pages close. A lantern
Shuttles through a cold like wires. A far
Off farm. What was the word? Darkness
Searches the earth, a million valleys,
A million streets, moving a finger
Over and over its chart, nearer
And near, and near circles, stalks him,
Rims wine glass-wise his skull and whistles.

That morning above Metapontum,
Of such a green of storm marine the
Such a hand upon the such a granite,
The icy line of rhythm, aloof
And rigid, the cleaving hieratic
Gesture of all his known, all his owned
Universe. There in a time of level
Light, an air in which the motes of music
Suspend uninterrupted in the
Imagination, in the beams of
Blue and gold sound, in the announcement

The fall of guided lambent water,
Of the presence of learned instruments,
An atmosphere where substance becomes
A visible dance, where the gilded,
Spun and polished acrobat explores
The flying vectors of harmonic range,
Frail cascaded parallelograms,
Bladed gulls up over grey old seas,
Lipped winds risen in Orion's swift
Geometries, horizon mountains
Kissing the curving cheek secluded
In gardens dense with perfume, in those
Tangents of living masks like comets
Which never escape the centripetal
Architects of memory—this girl
Who said, "My life is bought and paid for,
So much pleasure for so much pain."
The unkempt boy who said, "My mind slips
Through my fingers like Crusoe's doubloons
On his desert island." The aging
Gent who sucked his yellow teeth and said,
"I want life visible only through
The delicate anastomosis
Of the little bright red nerves of sex,"
In its very own Ten Towns of Troy,
The brain encapsulate like an onion jewel,
And Jason in his black ship in the
Phosphorescent coral sea under
The hidden moon, Jason or Gauguin,
Dun camels in the smoky desert,
The Pyramids gone crimson into time.
Things known are nice, worlds long remembered,
Ears attuned to catch from sliding thought
The slightest harmonies of ordered
Music of objects worn by careful hands.

So the slim loaf held in her bland hands,
Hair as blonde as mown rice, the simple
Newly domesticated flowers,
The lucent wine, olive oil, honey,

Figs, dry cheese, and fish, and pickled squid,
Accumulated in the movements
Of her wise body the pulse of China,
Of Ganges, and the painted Persian
Corridors, of all the long days danced
With military grace, and lived with
Caution and expectant beauty in
The Golden City at Crotona,
Milk of goat and cow and sheep, fruit and
Oil of the olive, honey and wheat,
White wool and dyes from the sea to dye
It, and fruit and juice of the grape.
These have entered her and garbed her, formed
The aura and measure of her movement.
Object by object, with poetic
Precision, recollection awakes
Note by memorable note of quiet
Song. So having broken bread beneath
The white pillars he rose and left the hill
To walk the sea strand of sculpt and colored
    stones and shells.

IV

THE STIGMATA OF FACT

This calcined idiocy, the fool
Naked and white in the night, the chalk
Old skull breaks, and breaks into weeping.
Tears water the roots of the living,
The pale lewd beast, Death's little chum, breaks
Into tears, corrupt and obscure tears.
We discovered on the last morning
Of the dig, at the very bottom
Of the excavation, the record
Of disgrace and dismay. We knew he
Was only hiding, shattering tears

Over our heads like clattering steel.
The sky was like the blue belly of
A boiler. The sun went over it
With hammers. Everything was present.
It was only a horn protruding
From the alkali crust, a relic
Of the days when the bison were here.

No matter where the spirit goes or
Goes out, the flesh will stay here, mixed with
This place, So many molecules, so
Many hairs in the head and mustache.
So many movements and no more, out
Of what might seem a most capacious
Infinitude. A piece of landscape
At Damascus. A smile in the
Gorgon's face rooted in only one
Instant as no mountain can ever
Be—gracious or anguished acceptance—
But rooted and fixed and no cavil.

One day as we were approaching one
Of the lesser islands, a barren
Place of burnt rock, which we all knew was
Uninhabited, we heard across
The water a great commotion like
A crowd of weeping women and then
A voice crying out, "Tammuz! Tammuz!"
There was a fellow on board called Thomas
And so for a joke he answered them,
"What do you want with me?" and the voice
Came back saying, "When you come to Crete,
Tell them there that the unknown god is dead."
It was a funny thing to happen
Nowadays on a dirty stinking
Tub like that. I never heard
What happened to the Thomas fellow
When we got to Crete, although I thought
I saw him once along the harbor,
His hat pulled over his eyes in an

30

Awful sun, watching a gang unloading goats.
A crumbling kingdom, a leper king,
Halls, banners, swords, and better plumbing
Than anything in Europe and silks
For all the women to wear all the time,
Up or in bed, impregnable forts
In the desert garrisoned by thieves,
Assassins everywhere, no street is safe,
In the country we travel only
With armed escort. Krak of Moab
Like a stone battleship in the desert.
"At last we have worn out our welcome."
Tammuz, the envoy of Alamut,
Smiles, sympathetic, reminiscent,
And noncommittal. Let the Graal pass.
Keep silence—the word is not worth giving.
The leper king lies in a bed all
Covered with purple and pall. Tammuz
Parts the arras, smiles again, farewell,
And goes across the drawbridge through the
Orchards, past the jousting and polo
Field, into the hazy hills dim with
Dust, his burnoose drawn across his face.

Dust—the turning years bring once again
In a hundred years exploring feet
To stir dust in one narrow sunbeam,
Dry choking dust, once each hundred years
A cough and sneeze, and then the thick dust
Settles once more on the disordered
Bones in their endless sleep, and the sand
Drifts against the doorway, nearer the
Lintel year by year. The law by which
We live is the law by which we die.
The rose breasted grosbeak obscured by
Flowering dogwood bloomed in the eye,
A sweet vertigo bloomed in the brain.
Her sex was moist, her mouth full of night.
At this point the peaks show best above
The valley through the trunks of the yellow pines.

Thomas looked at the pale blue snow peaks
And thought of the long crash of emirate
And corporation, the Caliph hiding
In some foetid desert tent, the ships
Of Royal Dutch Shell in the Malacca
Straits, or the others, the immortal
Element in an otherwise all
Dissolving corruption, the germ plasm
Of history. Here in this brilliant
Summer region, his painted landscape,
Thomas says, "There is no self subsistent
Microcosm." He thinks a while of
Chuang Tzu fishing with a straight pin and
Says, "There is no self subsistent
Macrocosm either."

                    The Old Man
Told Sebastian, "Everybody wants
To make that gruesome exploring trip
Sometime. The stone blocks are bigger than
A horse and every figure is life size
And plated with gold. Some of the galleries
Are like an aquarium, full of
Fish and octopuses, mostly though
It's bulls and naked women wiggling
In the torch light. The gold is as red
As blood in the torch light. It's quite a
Sight. A lot of fellows and girls
Come here from Athens on their honeymoons.
They are always shocked at the way our
Women paint and our men use perfume.
Some of them come back again and again.
Last week we had a couple on their
Golden wedding. Used to, you could hire
A guide, but they put a stop to that."

Sebastian said, "I am the master of the
Pattern of my life, freedom
Is the knowledge of necessity."
That evening when her act was over

She said, "My mother's sick. I've got to
Go see her." She sat in the cab
Calling her flesh back from the public,
Squeezing the orchestra out of it
And offering it to him. They bought
Some things to take. Self conscious for once,
Sebastian stood like a movie gent in the gas
Lit cubicle. The hamper on the
Single kitchen chair. A Sacred Heart
And an old calendar with "The Lone Wolf"
On the walls. The old Negress like a
Scrap of lumber under the thin cover.
Huge candy eyes wet with admiration.
The face like plum colored wood in the gas light.
She was obviously dying and
Going to be very hard to kill.
Circumstance had embalmed her long ago.
The most industrious worm would never
Penetrate her, no corruption take
Her dead as none could take her living.
Maxine fed her fried chicken and a
Hot peach fried pie and black eyed peas.
She was too weak to sit. Sebastian
Held her propped up, the one hard pillow
In his lap. They left her with a cup
Of steaming coffee laced with gin on
The chair beside her bed. "She's pretty
Sick," Sebastian said. "How long has she
Been this way?" Maxine said, "A couple
Years." They danced together, to the same
Band on the phonograph, in her flat.
She said, "I want to do my act just
For you, like I can never do it
In the club. I'll do it wonderful."

The five forerunners of cognition
Pause where the paths tangle in the wood.
They wait, naked and panting, startled.
Nothing moves along the forest trails.
The grass spreads over the meadows like

Green butter sprinkled with sequins.
Virgins came here with wicker baskets
To sing and pick the spangled flowers.
In the high mountain meadows wild goats
And mountain sheep bound over the rocks.
The bear ambles and the fox trots where
The light hangs like a high fog in the
Far off tree tops. Birds pulsate in the
Light. These athletes were cut by cleaner
Hands than Myron's. The man who did them
Is the man who sculpt the Minotaur.
Let no man to the hierosgamos
Of these minds admit impediment.

It might have been a gnarled dark rabbi
Sitting there, or an accident of
High tide and driftwood, down the beach there
In a whorl of sticks and feathers, bones
And dried out seaweed. It huddled there.
The fog left, blowing in over the land.
The blind eye of the sea and the blind
Rabbi exchanged stares. Sebastian had
No question. Far down some men
Were poking at the sea. Nearby, birds
Scratched it as it ran away from them.
This was not the Argonauts' water
But it wasn't a great deal different.
Sebastian said, "Do I possess this?
Or do I repossess myself? Dead?
No, living with a limitless sterile
Kind of life." Sebastian lay naked,
Blind, salty, and relaxed on the edge
Of the blind sea alone with the blind rabbi.

Morphology repeats ontology.
Thomas drank all night and read John of the Cross.
He was drunk and forsaken before
Dawn. At daylight he went out through the
Lion Gate and bought a ticket for
Knossos, where the women paint their breasts

34

And the men use perfume and the girls
Mate with bulls. The crowd boiled around him,
Lonely as beasts in a slaughter house.
The period grew blackly backward
Across its sentence. Theseus died
At last in a vulgar brawl. The priests,
Stinking of perfume, got him ready.
Why these overstained contortionist
Tricks? Archaeologists have proved
The Minotaur a lie, the labyrinth
A vast grocery store, Knossos so mild
It went unwalled. Even the Easter
Island anthropoliths were harmless
Statues of the royal kinfolks. Near
To us, nearer than the lamps that lit
The ceilings of Altamira and Dordogne,
The uncanny geomorphous companions wait—
Maybe, but today his theromorphs
Have outlasted every Pharaoh.

Saturday night, rain falls in the slums.
Rain veils the tired hurrying faces,
Sordid and beautiful in the rain.
Sebastian walks, puzzled, in the rain.
This is the macrocosm, on these
Materials it subsists. And the
Microcosm—This is the very thing.
There is no self that suffers rebirth.
Few trigliths of Stonehenge still stand there
In that immense windy nightbound plain.
It is cold after the summer rain.
"This is the place," she says, "Let's eat here."
She turns against him, warm and firm, rain
On her brown cheeks and odorous hair.
When he got home his cheeks were bronze, too,
As though with fever rather than sun,
His beard grizzled, his hair thinner.
The old dog discovered him and died.
The evil rivals died. The web flew wide.
And this was the little brother, the

Holy comedian, offering
Him the password at which all rusted
Hinges fall. This is the place where knowledge
Was so close to poplars and to stones.

Thomas looks out over the valley.
Far off in the low mists and fireflies
The lights along the railroad track change.
Then the whistle comes as distant as
A star and finally the distant
Roar and like a diamond necklace falling
Through the long somber valley the lighted
Cars, pulsating and slipping away
And the headlight twisting into the
Dimness like a cold needle. All so
Far away, not like a toy train but
Like some bright micro organism,
The night train to Omaha goes by.
Then Thomas quiets the zebra dun,
Tends the bannock and the tea and turns
The bacon. Grey low shapes of night bulk
Slow and make their own horizon. White
Ash flakes fall from the heart of the fire.
Now far, now near, the chuck-will's-widows
Call. Thomas smokes and spits into the
Fire. Bats cry, the creaking of the hundred,
Tiny, closing doors of silence.

A PROLEGOMENON
TO A THEODICY
(1925–1927)

For
Mildred
Andrée

A PROLEGOMENON
TO A THEODICY

a

This the mortared stone
Heated
The green lying over
The tinsel white that ascends
The rocker
Aboard aboard
It rustles rustles
Should he acquiesce to forever flow
No one shall ever enervate this structure
Where the worm walks
The fatigued worm
The countless green multiple umbrellas
And the red vestments
The toy balloons
Slowly it shifts all the lions grey
Shall you. Lion.
When you were young they called you Lilith
When you were young
It goes around it lies off
This is a squash
Thunder
More thunder
Still more
The little steel keys
Lock and revolve
And lock but
It is black scarred
Of what it was
When it stops transparent on the screen
Fish
Black

b

Has it been
No or has it
.alpha .gamma
The parallelogram of forces
The wishing cry the wishing
Is there a hole there where you walk or is there
Nothing
Is there an eyeball was it a demand or was it
A gift
In which nothing was given
Little planes of pain inserted in the brain
Needles in the tongue
"when you asked for it did you get it
were they many were they hard"
Remember that I told you there is nothing to
Be afraid of
I said there is nothing
I said it is a ghost it is a dream a
Joke an ontological neurosis
I told over and over
I said there is nothing
It is not an abyss
It is not even
a pit
Hope and hope muscle and muscle
O the pressure it presses o to get away to get
Away where it doesn't press where it isn't
Always pressing and pressing
Can't you understand
Can't you just forget and just believe believe
What. Believe
Nothing
Just believe
Living
Be
Be living   it is not even a pity nor the other thing
You think it is
If it was as you think someone would have
Told you o yes by now someone would
Don't you think someone would

c

The bell any bell and ring
The gold curves that wind up over the gold
The far shimmer
The exfoliate pentacles
The barging nosing lurging
Heave heavy
The dark
The cope of flesh the amethyst morse of pain
The unobtained ostensorium
They erected a sign
They said this is a sign
This is our own heraldry
In this way do we divide color from color
And it spreads it spreads over the sky the leaves
Of the canna
Wine brown o unanswered typhoon
Take a coarse comb and comb your vermicular throat
The red flowers that bleach in the sun
The roar crossed by the fine wires
In the haze the golden cumuli approach invisibility
The undersides of the forearms turn up
The lines on the palms shift like a graph of eels
It goes down down without alteration
With a chipper
Chirr
Down

d

I think secretly
Could it have for all the world have been just that
How have the blanketed eyes
Sensation drains through the body
The plague of grasshoppers blown out to sea, drowned,
    washed ashore heaps of them ten feet high rotting on
    miles of coast, stench in the air far inland
And one razor branch of bamboo in the sunlight in the
    twitter
As speaks the *cor anglais* the banal stab
And piston swims the air
The lucid crystal breaks always and recedes quanta

By quanta retreating
Engine of revelation
The beauty which was not otherwise than we could believe
As speaks the celesta
As speaks the ineffable triangle
The note which could never be interrupted and would
    never stop
O merle. O. O.   O. O. O.   O.
The gnomom falls erratic on the tangled thicket
The odor of raspberries crushed in the hot sun
Apparition
A mouthful of sticks and dactyls
It should be observed that this principle leads unavoidably
    to endless regress
We ferry the Skagit pulling ourselves along a cable
The mountains are purple and grey the valley is green the
    river is white
Milk of glaciers
In Horseshoe Basin the snow bled as the horses crossed it
A snarl of leaves
The curve of flesh
Evening and a light
I walk in the sunset
I walk in the sunrise
In the meantime I have been up all night
I have seen at a speed of three hundred kilometers a second
    the great nebula of Andromeda rushing upon me
The acoluthic sensation is still with me
The procession of cynocephali
Hysteresis   the shattered stone

      e

I told you how it was
I keep telling you over and over how it
Is
It is so easy to tell it over and over it is
So hard to get you to believe me
I take scenes I take places I say now isn't
This true
And this yes and this yes   yes

Yes   I don't know what else to say but
I want something else
I want and want always wear and wear
Always
Always
But you can't have it don't you realize there
Isn't any more there isn't any more at all not
At all
Greedy orphan of life
The bones are not broken the infinitely fine
Brain pan is still full to the pulsing
And there you stand "sad thin a trifle withdrawn"
And you stay that way
It isn't the way to stay
You ask presents
Surprise packages
What have you brought
Have you brought anything
Will you ever bring anything
Go into the sterile mountains into the region
Of minute stone
The puma that circles the pyramidal peaks
The eyes that dry revolve
Can you ask and after returning
Is it the same sewing and humming a little
Tune a little tumrtumrtumtumtum
O wise in moan
O infinitely wise and bent
And bowed and in the heart bowed down
Just born to die
Nobody will ever know anything about it
And I have nothing more at all to say.

          II

We were interested in ways of being
We saw lives
We saw animals
We saw agile rodents

Scala rodent
The harmonic pencil
Scala rodent
Emits its fundamental
The stricken plethora
A bottle of water against a very blue sky
A toppling shutter
The final peninsulas of space
Germinate in the secret ovoid perimeter
e.g.: scholia
The white hill
Elastic fatigue
The white lax hill and immediately the iced antelope
The line warps
The meridian of least resistance ascends the sky
The brain ferments
The curdled brain
The repercussion
The bullweaver
Obsessed by an ideograph
A mechanical bracelet
A small diesel engine
First one and then the other
Air congeals in water
The mural rift
A kind of going
The little block falls
The little wooden block
That long snarl of coast on the Mediterranean
The heart inclines
The four triangles
The fifth
The fingers jerk
The green cheek
The fourth
The image in the portal
The resin curls
The soggy mitten
The third
The cleaved cough

44

The second
The closing ribs
The first
The double envoi
The grackle breaks
Sweat
The diverse arrows
The anagogic eye

III

This is the winter of the hardest year
And did you dream
The white the large
The slow movement
The type of dream
The terror
The stumble stone
The winter the snow that was there
The neck and the hand
The head
The snow that was in the air
The long sun
The exodus of thought
The enervated violin
The oiled temples
The singing song and the sung
The lengthy home
The trundling endless stairs
The young stone
Homing and the song
The air that was there
Flayed jaws piled on the steps
The twirling rain
And laying they repeat the horizon
Ineffably to know how it goes swollen and then not swollen
Cold and then too warm
So many minor electrocutions

So many slaps of nausea
The keen eyelids
The abrupt diastole
That leaves you wondering
Why it was ever despite their assurances unlocked
Stars like lice along the scalp
The brain pan bitten burning
And dull on one foot
And dull on one foot
O cry aloud
O teeth unbound
Don't you know that the stone walk alone
Do you know the shredded brow
Are you aware
Do you take this forever concentric bland freezing to touch
Let the scarlet rustle
Let the globes come down
Let the oblate spheroids fall infinitely away
Forever away always falling but you can always see them
The creak
The squeak that makes you so slightly open your mouth
Patiently to be strangled
It is gone away somewhere
It is Winter
Reason
Winter
Ache

IV

Black
Blue black
Blue
The silver minuscules
In early dawn the plume of smoke
The throat of night
The plethora of wine
The fractured hour of light

The opaque lens
The climbing wheel
The beam of glow
The revealed tree
The wine crater
The soft depth
The suspended eye
The clouded pane
The droning wing
The white plateau
The hour of fractured light
The twisted peak
The cold index
The turquoise turning in the lunar sky
The climbing toe
The coastwise shout
The cracking mirror
The blue angle
The soothed nape
The minute flame
The silver ball
The concave mirror
The quivering palm
The conic of the wing
The trough of light
The rattling stones
The climbing humerus
The canyon bark
The unfolding leaves
The rigid lamp
The lengthy stair
The moving cubicle
The shifting floor
The bending femur
The rigid eye
The revealing lamp
The crackling anastomosis
The initial angle
The involved tendon
The yellow light

The acoluthic filaments
The general conic of the wing
The revealing eye
The crazed pane
The revelation of the lamp
The golden uncials
The revelation of the mirror

V

It is now a decline
A decline and an understanding
A shining water
A voiced multitude
A broken alphabet
The avian corpse

The little birds

The reeling breath
The colored leaves

The hills
The dark arch
The lowest rhythm
Opaqueness

The white stone

The tapers
Call

The pieces
The nostrils

Stoning
Striping nerves
The clicked eyes
The mill stone
Coruscate
She returns

The knuckles
The point of jaw

The tiring touch
Solace sometime
The living palm

The passing year

Ye that by night stand in the
house of the Lord

Lift up your hands in
   the sanctuary
                        And praise the Lord
The Lord that made   Heaven and earth
Blessing out of Sion   Give thee
Sicut erat
No cancelled brow   In principio
                        Peace says
Et nunc
Velvet   Peppermint
Spinning silver   Et semper
                        The beauty
Et in saecula   Cras amet
Saeculorum   Amavit
Qui nunquam   Vale
Veil   Saeculorum

         VI

         a

Asking is
Dream of deign
A coming so a come sowing
Day of drain
Leap of light
Strain strain the pinguid night long and told on sacrosanct
And told on **drought**
Song bell
Now sweep
Now ask
Dive glass. aside and lean
To the process the point comes the marching point the
      rocking icons all the flare of dark the recross and cross
      of waters underground
Hung white on that black
Agios
The crackling black   *o theos*
Qui labia Isaiae Prophetae calculo mundasti ignito

b

The germ of gold
Old
The story said. the moving waters
The illimitable thought that grows enlarges beyond the
    possibility of horizons
Forever going over the grey
Clasp soft and deign
Apollo moved
The air of flutes
Atalanta and the germ of gold
Persephone the germ of parchment red the granular carbon
    chromosomes
Between the eye and spiral thought the ceiling of the eye
The photosphere of buds
Of ice
Of leaves of gold
Is this the question
Is this the chute threat mountain
The crumbling femur
>   *Though the tree die and wither, whence*
>   *The apricots were got.*

c

Bubbles bitten by the chalky teeth
Lantern of the incessant sands
Grace encapsulate of grace unfolds
As
The chorded arc of eyes
Day of drain
Dire glass
The nerves in the cheek extinguished one by one psalm by
    psalm
The tenebrae of breath
Agios
The theory handed down from the Pythagoreans appears to
    have the same import. For some of this school maintain
    that the sunmotes in the air are the soul . . .
>   *Agios*
>   . . . others that

The soul is the principle which sets these in motion
Ischyros
Nostalgia of the tongue
Grey water
The shuttling barge
Air of gold
The floating egg
White
> *But as to the knowledge of the Word and of the things
> beheld in the Word, he is never in this way in
> potentiality. He is always actually beholding the Word
> and the things seen in the Word. For the bliss of Angels
> consists in such vision and beatitude, and does not
> consist in habit but in act, as the Philosopher says.*

d

Square
Agios ischyros
The stricken flint
The tongs of name
Athanatos
The trefoil flame
Nostalgia of the throat
Lumen Christi
The oldest oak
Bracken
Deo gratias
Sursum corda
Extraordinary cube sugar multiple retroactive fragments
Habemus ad Dominum
The every presence whirl
The spinning eye
The deepest air
The shadow lain across the noonday air
Eleison imas
The single wing
And the feather forever floating a thin spiral down forever
    in the air of noon

VII

a

The casual reverberation is not restitution
The doing must claim
A claimed doing
As there are passages in ambivalence
As the passage to Canopus
As the transit of residing
As the bifurcation that will never equalize
Shall we commit mitosis as mayhem, in the dark
And as you spoke they spoke
The gongs of name
Confusing a difficulty
(a difficult memorandum: a difficulty)
Eroding the essential plethora
The epact of the minute brain
Bargaining answers
Bargaining music
Stave sanctity
The upright eyes
The pole of light
Stave eyes
Audible folding that cannot watched sheds dichotomies
Stars burst
Jaws squirm beneath the ingrained claw
Eyes break the capsules of the strange arithmetics in claps
    of light
Stave eyes
And then to square the black square and the placental
    necessity in a stone acre
In a paralyzed night

b

Evasion is not contradiction
Aside is not against
This is that method
This one is aside
This one is against

Two
Oppose two
There is that trend
It is not enough to go posting in causes
It is not accurate to ask
It is not the case
Is the cause
Accepting collapsible perimeters to enquire
To encourage
To evolve differences
The partition of Athanasius
The partition of Sabellius
Now is the time and we go aside and they go away
The geminal eyes separate
The armature warps
Nothing to be avoided was disowned because nothing
     expected was expected
In all cases the concomittant values will always separate in
     such a way that the postulates gone to their creating
     will remain forever separated
Is the cause
Is the answer
To survey avenues of approximation may be held sufficient
     in more primitive organizations
The compass of two constants
Nothing under the only necessity will suffice
Not growing
Not doing

                  c

Doing is doing (doing as doing)
Nothing unwound
Evasion is consistent in equals
Evasion is pleasant on occasion
Green is green
That is, when there are polarities there is a pole, at least
     there is a polarizing activity
If there is not a necessity it does not mean that such a
     necessity is an impossible necessity. It means there are
     equals. It means there is measure in occasion

It is at least that
Green is green
When the activity is circular it means a center
When there are vortices it means at least an eye, it may
    mean a hand, it may mean germination
As a spiral
It is not always possible to suppose configuration
It is not even always possible to suppose intensification
It is not possible to suppose signification
Something
The cause is the case
Not in this place
The simultaneous cause is not however the perfect
    simultaneous case
Not perfect in this place
The fusion of Athanasius
The fusion of Sabellius
Now is the time for reversal of position in height
The crumbs of iron crawl
The beam bends
Perhaps if you were given one rubber neurone and then went
    far away it could be said: this is the case, likewise: this
    is the cause, as in the economy of a microcosmos there
    exist polar and antipolar determinants.

VIII

The grammar of cause
The cause of grammar
The being of grammar
The place of being
The magnificent being of division
The gradient of change
The invisible triangle of difference
Of division
The parsed challenge
If the extended injunction remains it will be almost possible
    to observe the dispersion of the closing and unclosing
    follicles

A constellation of difference
The constellations of stimuli
The binder bent
As death by night by sleep
The humor of not being
The periodic variation which descends like a curtain of cold
    fire from the aurora borealis
Commutative and optative eclipsed by an invisible
    companion
Spun on an harmonic ladder
Even the most primitive elements of consciousness will be
    seen to emerge as concepts
The cold tangle of bowels slides on itself
"Hunting badgers by owllight"
The curtain of glow bends on itself
The unnumbered thuribles will clink and the suave etiologic
    fog go up from the exterior world
Those worlds that bloom against the blessing retina,
    etiolate across unnumbered distances and disgulphing
    years
Hunting owls by flint light as with noiseless vibratory
    insistence the vast hieroglyphic machine traces the
    great and little lines of conscience
And "Faith sits triumphant on a car of gold
Of Tubal's making, where blew sapphires shine"
Of Tubal's, that is, the discipline of severed choice from
    satellite to sepulcher
As: "the choice of death rather than dishonorable wealth
    reveals character, the choice of a nectarine rather than
    a turnip does not."

IX

a

The bell
Too softly and too slowly tolled
And the first wave was snow
The second ice
The third fire
The fourth blood

The fifth adders
The sixth smother
The seventh foul stink
And unnumbered beasts swam in the sea
Some feather footed
Some devoid of any feet
And all with fiery eyes
And phosphorescent breath
The enduring bell
The wash of wave
The wiry cranes that stagger in the air
The hooded eyes struggling in the confused littoral
The smoky cloak
Those who walk
Those who are constrained
Those who watch the hole of wavering dark
There is no order in expectation
The feet fall
Even the enemy of cold labor
Of the mighty tongue
The gull matted on the sand
Worms spilling out of the beak
The cervical agony
Unplumbed and unforgotten caves
A cry sent up in expectation
A mouth filling the sky
Shaping the words of the victor
The bell
A voice
Blessed are the dead who die
The generations of generations

b

They were in an unstable condition
Floating about in a putrid fog
Throughout the tangled forest
Between the charred trunks
Over the yellow marshes
Some squirmed after the manner of lizards
Some were upright with their arms held up

Some lay with their knees partly drawn up
Some lay on their sides
Some lay stretched at full length
Some lay on their backs
Some were stooping
Some held their heads bent down
Some drew up their legs
Some embraced
Some kicked out with arms and legs
Some were kneeling
Some stood and inhaled deep breaths
Some crawled
Some walked
Some felt about in the dark
Some arose
Some gazed, sitting still

c

Imperceptible light
Scintilla animae
In slumber behold the compass swinging
Behold the man swung in the way
The early meditation
The morning light in the throat
And the shield hung from the lintel
Swayed in the wind
Slowly the immense creaking screw
Turns
Nor the canker
Turns
Nor the entangled bone
Turns
Nor the salt of the sea
Turns
Nor the broken glass
Turns
Only a sudden confusion
Turning
And the secret appearance of the twilight lion
Turning

57

The hands clutching the knees
The bloody ankles
Which might devour
Which might trample
Which shall dissolve in the hands
And the instruments
And the broken gate
And a small light
The bent woman who admits the visitor with questions
The throat dry and dust in the hair
He sees him alive
The tired men converse watching the wrestlers
     under the arc-light
You stand in the house at night

X

a

In those days
In a pool of noise
Down the unending staircase goes the mother who shall
    not die till she finds her daughter
The winding labor
The well of lost destinations
He that is comely when old and decrepit surely was very
    beautiful when he was young. And he considered that
    they who had fallen asleep with godliness had great
    grace laid up for them, for their works follow them.
    Beneath the heavy trees in an ivory chair dozed the
    master of those who know.
Now it would be useless for a thing to be moved unless it
    were able to reach the end of that movement, hence
    that which has a natural aptitude for being moved
    towards a certain end must needs be able to reach
    that end.
A traveller who has lost his way should not ask, Where am
    I? What he really wants to know is, where are the
    other places? He has his own body, but he has lost them.
An Aristotle was but the rubbish of an Adam and Athens
    but the rudiments of Paradise.

b

The torch
At that time
The bell
At that hour
Throughout the obscure machine
The slow unlocking and locking shifts
The blue gleams stir
The stellar vectors converge on the microscopic paradigm
Behold the man Gabriel, whom I had seen in the vision at
     the beginning, flying swiftly touched me at the time
     of evening sacrifice.
A movement athwart the gradients of thought
The larvae of the brain
A song in the peace of sleep
The larval brain
The rhythmic bell
The vested day
At that hour
The angel Gabriel seized the evil spirit and tied it up in
     the desert of upper Egypt

c

He descends five hundred steps
They hear his breathing secretly
The murmur of the midnight air
The unendurable fragrance
O woe unto him
The breath of God
The embowelled wanderers
The spark
Light by night to travellers
Remembering happiness
Separating night from night
Hearest thou what curious things all the caves of night
     answer
The bright leaves reflect the severe light
Is the labor lost
The ululating she-goat
The cloud of sparks

The manifold bars of gold
The broom of light
The sweeping glow
The burnished ladders of the intellect
The silver spiral of the will
Tense in the telic light

d

Light
Light
The sliver in the firmament
The stirring horde
The rocking wave
The name breaks in the sky
Why stand we
Why go we nought
They broken seek the cleaving balance
The young men gone
Lux lucis
The revolving company
The water flowing from the right side
Et fons luminis
The ciborium of the abyss
The bread of light
The chalice of the byss
The wine of flaming light
The wheeling multitude
The rocking cry
The reverberant scalar song lifts up
The metric finger aeon by aeon
And the cloud of memory descends
The regnant fruitful vine
The exploding rock
The exploding mountain cry
Tris agios
The sapphire snow
Hryca hryca nazaza

THE PHOENIX AND
THE TORTOISE
(1940–1944)

For
Marie

THE PHOENIX AND
THE TORTOISE

I

Webs of misery spread in the brain,
In the dry Spring in the soft heat.
Dirty cotton bolls of cloud hang
At the sky's edge; vague yellow stratus
Glimmer behind them. It is storming
Somewhere far out in the ocean.
All night vast rollers exploded
Offshore; now the sea has subsided
To a massive, uneasy torpor.
Fragments of its inexhaustible
Life litter the shingle, sea hares,
Broken starfish, a dead octopus,
And everywhere, swarming like ants,
Innumerable hermit crabs,
Hungry and efficient as maggots.

This is not the first time this shingle
Has been here. These cobbles are washed
From ancient conglomerate beds,
Beaches of the Franciscan series,
The immense layer cake of grey strata
That hangs without top or bottom
In the geological past
Of the California Coast Ranges.
There are no fossils in them. Their
Dates are disputed—thousands of feet,
Thousands and thousands of years, of bays,
Tidemarshes, estuaries, beaches,
Where time flowed eventless as silt.
Further along the beach the stones
Change; the cliffs are yellow with black
Bands of lignite; and scattered amongst
The sand dollars in the storm's refuse

Are fossil sand dollars the sea
Has washed from stone, as it has washed
These, newly dead, from life.

                    And I,
Walking by the viscid, menacing
Water, turn with my heavy heart
In my baffled brain, Plutarch's page—
The falling light of the Spartan
Heroes in the late Hellenic dusk—
Agis, Cleomenes—this poem
Of the phoenix and the tortoise—
Of what survives and what perishes,
And how, of the fall of history
And waste of fact—on the crumbling
Edge of a ruined polity
That washes away in an ocean
Whose shores are all washing into death.

A group of terrified children
Has just discovered the body
Of a Japanese sailor bumping
In a snarl of kelp in a tidepool.
While the crowd collects, I stand, mute
As he, watching his smashed ribs breathe
Of the life of the ocean, his white
Torn bowels braid themselves with the kelp;
And, out of his drained grey flesh, he
Watches me with open hard eyes
Like small indestructible animals—
Me—who stand here on the edge of death,
Seeking the continuity,
The germ plasm, of history,
The epic's lyric absolute.

What happened, and what is remembered—
Or—history is the description
Of those forms of man's activity
Where value survives at the lowest

64

Level necessary to insure
Temporal continuity.
Or "as the Philosopher says,"
The historian differs from
The poet in this: the historian
Presents what did happen, the poet,
What might happen. For this reason
Poetry is more philosophic
Than history, and less trivial.
Poetry presents generalities,
History merely particulars.
So action is generalized
Into what an essential person
Must do by virtue of his essence—
Acting in an imaginary
Order of being, where existence
And essence, as in the Deity
Of Aquinas, fuse in pure act.
What happens in the mere occasion
To human beings is recorded
As an occurrence in the gulf
Between essence and existence—
An event of marginal content.

In the artificially bright
Evening of the clocks of war,
In the last Passover of the just,
We too prepare symbolic supper.
The low fog coils across the sun,
And falls back, and the powerful
Gold Aton blades of the desert sun
Shine again on the desert land
And over the fogbound ocean.
One side of the canyon is frigid
With shadow, and the other busy
In the dense heat. I build the fire
At the stream's edge. The flames are pale
In the sunlight, thick and fleshy
In their reflections on the water.

While I wait for the water to boil,
I stand, abstract, one breathing man,
On the suture of desert, sea,
And running water brief as Spring.
Sagebrush and seaweed, sand and granite,
Mice and plankton, sterile and swarming,
Steam and spume, inhale and exhale—
Out of this the ancient Chinese
Built up their whole cosmology—
Rest that dissipates into motion,
And motion that freezes into rest.
And you ride up, hungry, shouting
For supper, on a red stallion,
Breasts quivering in their silk blouse.
Yin and Yang . . . possibly history
Is only an irritability,
A perversion of the blood's chemistry,
The after effects of a six thousand
Years dead solar cyclone.

                    In the twilight . . .
Here, on the soft unblemished skin,
Where ear and jaw and throat are joined,
Where a flush begins to spread
Under the glittering down;
Here, where the gracious eyebrow
Tapers over the orbit and onto the edge
Of the blue shadowed temple;
Here, on the lips curled back
To begin a smile, showing the teeth
And the tongue tip . . . kisses in the evening,
After supper on the anniversary
Of the white gift of sacramental flesh.

Of what body. Through what years. In what light.

Value and fact are polar aspects
Of organic process. As plus
Is to minus a value: "virtue"
And minus is privative "fact";

So minus is to virtue, "sin."
That is, quality is the aspect
Assumed in perspective of polar
Antitheses of achievement.
How comfortable, and how verbal.

The free laughter and the ivory feet
Treading the grapes—the tousled hair—
The dark juice rising between the thighs
Of the laughing, falling girl, spreading
Through the dark pubic hair, over
The laughing belly.

     The law by which
We live is the law by which we die.
Again, "as the Philosopher says,"
The ground of individuation
Is the ground of communication.
As pure potentials, the mistresses
Of Alexander and the bedmates
Of the perdurable fellahin
Return finally from history
To the common ground of all discourse.

Found in the smashed tent on Everest—
"Dear Noel,
    We'll probably start
early tomorrow (8th) in order
to have clear weather. It wont be
too early to start looking out
for us either crossing the neckband
under the pyramid or going
up to the skyline at 8 p.m.
yours ever,
    Geo. Mallory"

When process is defined as the field
Suspended between positive
And negative, the Absolute One
And the Absolute Many, the poles

Of being short circuit in reason.
The definition dissolves itself.
Anode and cathode deliquesce
By virtue of inherent structure.
Unavoidably the procedures
Of logic flatter the Deity.

Not want and fear, but the rigid
Vectors of the fallible mind
Confuse all pantheons and haunt
Geometries—and if not fear
And danger, then danger and desire.
Always the struggle to break out
Of the argument that proves itself,
Past procedure as perimeter,
Past the molecular landslide,
Past the centrifugal perspectives
Of precipitous gain and loss,
Past the attrition of estate . . .
On the frontiers, all boundaries fuse,
Peaks, passes and glaciers, kisses,
Lips and epistemologies.
And the wardens of ontology,
The lethal sophists and policemen,
Patrol the surveyed boundaries.
In the bistros and academies
Rhetoricians seek the absolute
Hallucination. In the bureaux
Of policy it is put in practice.
History is the chronicle
Of the more spectacular failures
To discover vital conflict.

Not want and fear, but danger and desire . . .
Contemporary mysticism
Accounts for all motivation
By the bitch's tit and the dropped pup.
(The vectors don't explain themselves.)
Well might the aging précieux cry out,

"Zénon! Cruel Zénon d'Elée!"
Or turgid Webster lucidly say,
"Like diamonds we are cut with our own dust."

Danger and desire, or jealousy
And fear of pain, the constant pressure
For the lesser, immediate, good . . .
The three tragedians saw lives
As strung on doom, like the lion's teeth
On his still tensile sinews;
Persons as trophies, the savage
Jewelry of continuity
From "pure function to pure potential,"
And Karma, the terrifying
Accumulation of bare fact.
And in dynamic antithesis,
The person as priest and victim—
The·fulfillment of uniqueness
In perfect identification,
In ideal representation,
As the usurping attorney,
The real and effective surrogate.

Iphigenia at Aulis—
The ritual person emerges
As term of responsibility.
Doom or responsibility—
Fashionable superstition builds
The world from "intervals at which
Accidents are likely to happen."
Catastrophic contingency
In physics or theology,
God as pure fiat, the person
As pure caprice, ends in the worship
Of history as demonic will,
The pandemic destroying Europe.

The lucid Socratic drama
Defines tragedy by example;

Aristotle's recipe book
Neglects to explain why tragedy
Is tragic, the hero, heroic.
Even the Angelic Doctor,
When he came to deal with angels,
That is, personality as such,
Produced the perfect anti-person.
Scotus—Luther—Kierkegaard—Barth—
The dark Gothic demonolatry,
Or the spotless imitation man,
One of David's noble lay figures—
The Oath of the Horatii —
The flesh made of highly polished lead.

The problem of personality
Is the problem of the value
Of the world as a totality,
The problem of immortality
As a basic category—
That passed away, so will this.
The moraine creeps on the meadow;
The temples dissolve in the jungle;
The patterns abide and reassert
Themselves; the texture wears through the nap.

All the terminals coalesce
In the region that defines reason.
In this wilderness as men say
Are the trees of the Sun and the Moon
That spake to King Alexander
And told him of his death.

                              And they took
The head of Bran, and came to Harlech
And the three birds of Rhiannon
Came and sang to them for seven years;
And it seemed as though the birds were far
Distant over the sea, and yet
They were clear, and distinct, and close.

And they went to Gwales in Penvro
To a kingly and spacious hall
That overlooked the sea. And the third
Door that looked towards Cornwall was closed.
And they placed the head in high honor,
And dined and drank and were happy,
And remembered none of their sorrow.
And after fourscore years, on a day,
Heilyn ap Gwynn opened the door
To see if Bran had spoken the truth.
And they looked out over Cornwall
And Aber Henvelen, and as they looked,
They saw all the evils they had suffered,
And all the companions they had lost,
And all the old misery, and the death
Of their good lord, all as though once again,
It was happening there, in that same spot.
And they could not stay, but went to London,
And buried the head in the White Mount.

The perfect circle. The perfect term.

Endurance, novelty, and simple
Occurrence—and here I am, a node
In a context of disasters,
Still struggling with the old question,
Often and elaborately begged.
The atoms of Lucretius still,
Falling, inexplicably swerve.
And the generation that purposed
To control history vanishes
In its own apotheosis
Of calamity, unable
To explain why anything
Should happen at all.

One more Spring, and after the bees go,
The soft moths stagger in the firelight;
And silent, vertiginous, sliding,

The great owls hunt low in the air;
And the dwarf owls speak at their burrows.
We walk under setting Orion,
Once more in the dim boom of the sea,
Between bearded, dying apple trees,
In the shadows of the Easter moon;
And silent, vertiginous, the stars
Slide over us past the equinox.
The flowers whirl away in the wind like snow.
The thing that falls away is myself.
The moonlight of the Resurrection,
The moon of Amida on the sea,
Glitters on the wings of the bombers,
Illuminates the darkened cities.
The motion of Egyptian chisels
Dissolves slowly in the desert noon.

It is past midnight and the faint,
Myriad crying of the seabirds
Enters my sleep. The wind rises.
I hear the unbelievably
Distant voices of the multitudes
Of men mewing in the thoroughfares
Of dreams. The waves crowd on the beach.
A log falls in the fire. The wind
Funnels the sparks out in the moonlight
Like a glowing tree dragged through dark.
I see in sudden total vision
The substance of entranc'd Boehme's awe:
The illimitable hour glass
Of the universe eternally
Turning, and the gold sands falling
From God, and the silver sands rising
From God, the double splendors of joy
That fuse and divide again
In the narrow passage of the Cross.

The source of individuation—
The source of communication—
Peace, the conservation of value—

Came Jesus and stood in the midst, and
Saith unto them, "Peace be unto you."
And when he had so said, he shewed
Unto them his hands and his side.

The fire is dense again in the dark.
I turn my face into shadow
And fall again towards sleep,

                              Amida,
Kwannon, turn from peace. As moonlight
Flows on the tides, innumerable
Dark worlds flow into splendor.

How many nights have we awakened—
The killdeer crying in the seawind.

II

I am cold in my folded blanket,
Huddled on the ground in the moonlight.

The crickets cry in congealing frost;
Field mice run over my body;
The frost thickens and the night goes by.

North of us lies the vindictive
Foolish city asleep under its guns;
Its rodent ambitions washing out
In sewage and unwholesome dreams.
Behind the backs of drowsy sentries
The moonlight shines through frosted glass—
On the floors of innumerable
Corridors the mystic symbols
Of the bureaucrats are reversed—
Mirrorwise, as Leonardo
Kept the fever charts of one person.
Two Ptahs, two Muhammad's coffins,
We float in the illimitable

Surgery of moonlight, isolate
From each other and the turning earth;
Motionless; frost on our faces;
Eyes by turns alive, dark in the dark.

The State is the organization
Of the evil instincts of mankind.
History is the penalty
We pay for original sin.
In the conflict of appetite
And desire, the person finally
Loses; either the technology
Of the choice of the lesser evil
Overwhelms him; or a universe
Where the stars in their courses move
To ends that justify their means
Dissolves him in its elements.
He cannot win, not on this table.
The World, the Flesh, and the Devil—
The Tempter offered Christ mastery
Of the three master institutions,
Godparents of all destruction—
"Miracle, Mystery, and Authority—"
The systematization of
Appetitive choice to obtain
Desire by accumulation.

History continuously
Bleeds to death through a million secret
Wounds of trivial hunger and fear.
Its stockholders' private disasters
Are amortized in catastrophe.

War is the health of the State? Indeed!
War is the State. All personal
Anti-institutional values
Must be burnt out of each generation.
If a massive continuum
Of personality endured
Into grandchildren, history
Would stop.

74

"As the Philosopher says,"
Man is a social animal;
That is, top dog of a slave state.
All those lucid, noble minds admired
Sparta, and well they might. Surely
It is highly questionable
If Plato's thesis can be denied.
The Just Man is the Citizen.
Wars exist to take care of persons.
The species affords no aberrants.

Barmaid of Syria, her hair bound
In a Greek turban, her flanks
Learnedly swaying, shivering
In the shiver of castanets,
Drunk, strutting lasciviously
In the smoke filled tavern . . .

What nexus gathers and dissolves here
In the fortuitous unity
Of revolving night and myself?
They say that history, defining
Responsibility in terms
Of the objective continuum,
Limits, and at the same time creates,
Its participants. They further say
That rational existence is
Essentially harmonic selection.
Discarding "is," the five terms
Are equated, the argument closed.
Cogito and Ergo and Sum play
Leapfrog—fact—process—process—fact—
Between my sleeping body and
The galaxy what Homeric
Heroes struggle for my arms?

Fact and value, process and value,
"Process, not result of judgment,"
Or, result, not process of judgment,
Or, judgment, not result of process,
Or, judgment of result, not process,

The possible combinations
Can be found by arithmetic
Or learned in the School of Experience.
The whalebone sieves the whale food
From the plankton, the plankton
Finally dissolves the whale,
Liberating the whalebone.
Liberty is the mother
Not the daughter of order.

Value evolves in decision;
History passes, pedetemtim;
The results of decision dissolve.
The assumption of history
Is that the primary vehicle
Of social memory is the State.

The nighthawks cry in the saffron
Twilight over the smoky streets
Of Chicago. It is Summer.
Victimae paschali, the wise
Jubilant melody of the
Easter Sequence breaks in the Mass.
The song of the monks is like laughter.
It is Spring, intense and sunlit.
The fieldpieces bang on the warped streets
Of Boston. Riots sweep over the world.
Midsummer—the harvest over.
The American polity
Discards its chrysalis of myth.
Ribbentrop and Stalin exchange smirks,
The fruit falls from the tree. Summer ends.

Was it Carnot who said, "The end
Justifies the means?" Or was it Marx?
Or Adams? "As teleology
Subsides to a minimum, achievement
Rises to a maximum." "The sum
Of conflagration is tepidity."
The infinitely cool, Virgin
Or Dynamo; the term: entropy

Or fecundity; the bleak Yankee
Purposiveness always gnawing:
"You have nothing to lose but your chains."
They are willing to pay any price.
They can be bought for any price.

As the Philosopher says,
That only is natural which contains
The principle of its own change within
Itself; what comes by chance is accident.
Being is statistical likelihood;
Actuaries conjure the actual.
In the words of the Stagirite,
"Nature comes apart at the joints."
Or, a theory of history,
"Physiologists and physicians
Have a fuller knowledge of the human
Body than the most anxious mother."

"The inhabitants of the world
At each successive period
In its history have beaten
Their predecessors in the race
For life, and are, in so far, higher
In the scale." So Darwin himself.
Natura non facit saltum.
The Franciscan series under me
Revolves with the planet, a mile thick
Mummy of blank catastrophe.

Gilbert White in his garden, Darwin
Poking around on the Beagle,
Franklin vanishing in the Arctic,
"There is no such thing as negative
Historical evidence."

The vast onion of the actual:
The universe, the galaxy,
The solar system, and the earth,
And life, and human life, and men's
Relationships, and men, and each man . . .

History seeping from capsule
To capsule, from periphery
To center, and outward again . . .
The sparkling quanta of events,
The pulsing wave motion of value . . .

Marx. Kropotkin. Adams. Acton.
Spengler, Toynbee. Tarn building empires
From a few coins found in a cellar . . .
History . . . the price we pay for man's
First disobedience . . . John of Patmos,
The philosopher of history.

This body huddled on the whirling
Earth, dipping the surface of sleep
As damsel flies sting the water's skin
With life. What is half remembered
In the hypnogogy of time;
Ineradicable bits of tune;
Nicias in rout from Syracuse;
Scarlet Wolsey splendid on the Field
Of the Cloth of Gold; More on trial;
Abélard crying for that girl;
"More than my brother, Jonathan,
Of one soul with me,
What sin, what pollution,
Has torn out bowels asunder."
The burnt out watch fires of Modena;
Or Phoebi claro—love, dawn, and fear
Of treacherous death; the enervated
Musical, dim edge of sleep;
Archdeacon Stuck on McKinley
Singing, "Te Deum laudamus . . ."
In the clenching cold and the thin air;
Lawrence dying of his body,
Blue gentians burning in the dark mind;
The conflict of events and change.

In their hour the constellations
Of Autumn mount guard over me—

Aquarius and Capricorn,
Watchers of my birth and of the turn
Of the apocalyptic future;
Noah and Pan in deadly conflict,
Watched by Fomalhaut's cold, single eye.
These are the stars that marched over
Boethius in meditation,
Waiting the pleasure of the Goth;
And once Chinese philosophers
Saw all the visible planets
In conjunction in Capricorn,
Two thousand, four hundred, forty-nine
Years before Christ.

             The thinne fame
Yit lasting, of hir ydel names,
Is marked with a fewe lettres . . .

Loken up-on the brode shewinge
Contrees of hevene, and up-on
The streit site of this erthe . . .

Liggeth thanne stille, all outrely
Unknowable; ne fame maketh yow
Not know.

III

Softly and singly an owl
Cries in my sleep. I awake and turn
My head, but there is only the moon
Sinking in the early dawn.
Owls do not cry over the ocean.
The night patrol planes return
Opaque against the transparent moon.
"The owl of Minerva," says Hegel,
"Takes her flight in the evening."
It is terrible to lie
Besides my wife's canvas chrysalis,

Watching the imperceptible
Preparation of morning,
And think that this probably is not
The historical evening we thought;
Waking in the twilight like bemused
Drunkards; but the malignant
Dawn of the literate insect,
Dispassionate, efficient, formic.

Irrelevant appetite dissolves
The neurones of a deranged nation—
Nucleus of alcohol, fibers
"Meandering in pellucid gold."
Remorse and guilt stiffen the tissues
With hypnotic dread of penitence.
Stone lodges against the heart
A blank total of catastrophe—
The bloody heart, suspicious
And ruined, but still the irritant
In the vitals of this iron mollusc,
Still the cause of its daily
Frightened secretions of mud.

The ant has perfect statistical
Intelligence, "a thoroughly
Humean approach to the problem
Of causality." History starts
With the dislocation of units,
The creation of persons,
A phenomenon of diffusion
In the high tension gap between
Technology and environment.
On the edges of riparian
Egypt and Mesopotamia
The dense family societal body
Acquired leucocytes within
And parasites without. "History
Is the instability
Of the family constellation."
Its goal is the achievement

Of the completely atomic
Individual and the pure
Commodity relationship—
The windowless monad sustained
By Providence. History
Ceases in a change of phase—
The polarization of its parts
In a supernatural kindred.

Shogun or Mikado—the Sun King
Eighteen centuries before Christ
Or after—amateur lockmakers
With pussy mistresses—the pure form
Of the cutting edge of power—
Man reduced to an entelechy—
"I lay down my pen in horror,
Not at the thought of Ivan's
Atrocities, but at the thought
That high minded, noble men
For years found it expedient
To bow to his will, to act
As instruments of his monstrous crimes."
"Politics is the art of choosing
The lesser evil." "The State, that's me."
Splendid as a rococo
Sunburst, with its powdered face buried
In the immortal buttocks
Of little Murphy, St. Thomas More
Or venereal Anne Boleyn—
Posterity in gratuity
Has provided both with beautiful
Apocryphal testaments.

The flow of interoffice
Memoranda charts the excretions
Of societal process,
The cast snakeskin, the fleeting
Quantum, Economic Man.
Novelty comes to be considered
The unpredictable, process

The clean columbarium
Of consumed statistical
Probabilities. Pascal
Merges with Hume; the stresses
Of the architecture are computed
By roulette; "the foundations
Are ingeniously supported
By the superstructure"; the agent
For insurance evicts that agent
Once thought more noble than the patient,
And his ontology along with him.
In the words of the Philosopher
King, Faustina's husband, "If I don't,
Somebody else will. Think of the good
I can do with my authority."
John Maynard Keynes visits the White House.

"Salvation equals autonomy."
All major religions have said so,
Whatever their founders thought.
Six thousand years of struggle
For autonomy, and what's to pay?
The terrified Phi Beta Kappas
Cower behind the columns
They afforded the masses,
Whispering, "E pluribus unum."
Or the Sufi, shrouded in white wool,
Meditating in dead Ctesiphon,
Spinning the erotic metaphors
Of self abandonment—wine, rubies
And perfumed buttocks—for the jackals
And cactus—the slow self destruction
Of the human, consumed away
By the inaccessible sun
Of absolute unity.

Hippias and Socrates
Contending for the title
Of Most Autonomous Greek.
Hippias who duplicated

The cube; who came to Olympia
With all that he had about
His body the work of his own hands—
A ring and seal, a strigil
And vanity case, high shoes and cloak,
And underwear, and a belt,
A perfect imitation
Of the finest Persian leather work;
Who came to Olympia
Carrying tragedies, dithyrambs,
Epics, learned treatises,
And all of his own composition,
Rhetorically sublime,
Grammatically immaculate,
Besides a system of mnemonics;
Who stood in public in all
The Greek cities and had an answer
For all questions; who came to Sparta
With a theory of the Beautiful
All his own, and many ingenious
Contrivances in mathematics,
And found a people interested
Only in archaeology
And history—their own history
And the ruins they had made elsewhere.
And Socrates, playing practical
Jokes on the imperium.
As the Philosopher says,
"All men desire to know." A highly
Undetermined appetite.

Atomization versus
Autonomy—the odds are with
The side with the most matériel.
The most resistant elements break
Under sixty centuries
Of attrition; only a species
Of hysteresis preserves
A sort of residue, overplus
Of past renunciation.

The saint becomes a madman,
The sage a crank, the beggar
A pauper, the courtesan
A whore or enthusiast.
Time's crystals lodge against the bitter
Heart at last, even the perfected
Heart of flesh.

Eva and Ave,
The swords of history—jealousy,
The fear of autonomous action,
The sharer of the gaudy apple
Of Atalanta and Paris,
Persephone's parchment red
Globule and its carbon chromosomes,
The germ of gold and the counter-heart;
And conversely, the hara-kiri
Sword of history, the goal
Of pure undetermined fiat,
Duns Scotus' Immaculate Virgin,
The sentimental climax
Of aged Goethe's vision,
"The form of the cutting edge—"
And as contradictory, Murphy
Cuddling that sword in tickles,
And lovely bemused Lesbia
Kneeling in every Roman alley.

And somewhere the irreducible
Fused unity and duality,
The fluent, liquid source of number.
The busy Myrmidons, those sly men,
Retreat to the last river,
The continuity of the germ plasm,
The animal tribute to a brief
Eternity. The Philosopher:
"Matter is the tendency
To immediate ends. An exact
And adequate material force
Must always deflect another force.

As the new form evolves, the prior
Recedes reciprocally into
Pure potentiality."

The institution is a device
For providing molecular
Process with delusive credentials.
"Value is the reflection
Of satisfied appetite,
The formal aspect of the tension
Generated by resolution
Of fact." Overspecialization,
Proliferation, gigantism.

Would it have been better to have slept
And dreamed, than to have watched night
Pass and this slow moon sink? My wife sleeps
And her dreams measure the hours
As accurately as my
Meditations in cold solitude.
I have lain awake while the moon crossed,
Dragging at the tangled ways
Of the sea and the tangled, blood filled
Veins of sleepers. I am not alone,
Caught in the turning of the seasons.
As the long beams of the setting moon
Move against the breaking day,
The suspended light pulsates
Like floating snow. Involuntary,
I may live on, sustained in the web
Of accident, never forgetting
This midnight moon that already blurs
In memory.
                    As certain
As color passes from the petal,
Irrevocable as flesh,
The gazing eye falls through the world.
As the light breaks over the water
One by one, pedetemtim,
The stakes of the nets appear

Stretching far out into the shallows,
And beyond them the dark animal
Shadow of a camouflaged cruiser.

IV

Dark within dark I cling to sleep,
The heart's capsule closed in the fist
Of circumstance; prison within
Prison, inseparably dark,
I struggle to hold oblivion
As Jacob struggled in a dream,
And woke touched and with another name.
And on the thin brainpan of sleep
The mill of Gaza grinds;
The heart condenses; and beyond
The world's lip the sun to me is dark
And silent as the moon that falls ·
Through the last degrees of night into
The unknown antipodes. I lie
At random, carelessly diffused,
Stone and amoeba on the verge
Of partition; and beyond the reach
Of my drowsy integrity,
The race of glory and the race
Of shame, just or unjust, alike
Miserable, both come to evil end.

Eventually history
Distills off all accumulated
Values but one. Babies are more
Durable than monuments, the rose
Outlives Ausonius, Ronsard,
And Waller, and Horace's pear tree
His immortal column. Once more
Process is precipitated
In the tirelessly receptive womb.

In the decay of the sufficient
Reasonableness of sacraments
Marriage holds by its bona fides.

Beneath what shield and from what flame.

The darkness gathers about Lawrence
Dying by the dead Mediterranean—
Catullus is psychoanalyzed
Between wars in lickerish London.
Another aging précieux
Drinks cognac, dreams of rutting children
In the Mississippi Valley,
Watches the Will destroy the logic
Of Christopher Wren and Richelieu.
Schweitzer plays Bach in the jungle.
It is all over—just and unjust.
The seed leaks through the gravel.

The light grows stronger and my lids
That were black turn red; the blood turns
To the coming sun. I sit up
And look out over the bright quiet
Sea and the blue and yellow cliffs
And the pure white tatters of fog
Dissolving on the black fir ridges.
The world is immovable
And immaculate. The argument
Has come to an end; it is morning,
And in the isolating morning
The problem hangs suspended, lucid
In a crystal cabinet of air
And angels where only bird song wakes.

"Value is the elastic ether
Of quality that fills up the gaps
In the continuum of discreet
Quality—the prime togetherness."
The assumption of order,

The principle of parsimony,
Remain mysteries; fact and logic
Meet only in catastrophe.
So long ago they discovered that
Each new irrational is the start
Of a new series of numbers;
Called God the source of systematic
Irrationalization of given
Order—the organism that
Geometricizes. And that vain
Boy, systematically deranging
Himself amongst the smoky cannoneers
Of the Commune, finding a bronze
Apotheosis as the perfect
Provincial French merchant who made good.
The statistical likelihood
Of being blown to pieces.

"Value is the reflection
Of satisfied appetite."
The State organizes ecstasy.
The dinosaur wallows in the chilling
Marsh. The bombs fall on the packed dance halls.
The sperm seeks the egg in the gravel.
"Novelty is, by definition,
Value-positive."

                    "Value
Is a phase change in the relations
Of events." Does that mean anything?

Morning. It is Good Friday Morning;
Communion has past to Agony
And Agony is gone and only
Responsibility remains; doom
Watches with its inorganic eyes,
The bright, blind regiments, hidden
By the sun-flushed sky, the remote
Indestructible animals.

Value, causality, being,
Are reducible to the purest
Act, the self-determining person,
He who discriminates structure
In contingency, he who assumes
All the responsibility
Of ordered, focused, potential—
Sustained by all the universe,
Focusing the universe in act—
The person, the absolute price,
The only blood defiance of doom.

Whymper, coming down the Matterhorn,
After the mountain had collected
Its terrible, casual fee,
The blackmail of an imbecile beauty:
"About 6 PM we arrived
Upon the ridge descending towards
Zermatt, and all peril was over.
We frequently looked, but in vain,
For traces of our unfortunate
Companions; we bent over the ridge
And cried to them, but no sound returned.
Convinced at last that they were neither
Within sight nor hearing we ceased;
And, too cast down for speech, silently
Gathered up our things and the little
Effects of those who were lost
And prepared to continue
The descent. When, lo! a mighty arch
And beneath it a huge cross of light
Appeared, rising above the Lyskamm
High into the sky. Pale, colorless,
And noiseless, but perfectly sharp
And defined, except where it was lost
In the clouds, this unearthly
Apparition seemed like a vision
From another world; and appalled,
We watched with amazement the gradual
Development of two vast crosses

One on either side . . . Our movements
Had no effect on it, the spectral
Forms remained motionless. It was
A fearful and wonderful sight;
Unique in my experience,
And impressive beyond description,
Coming at such a moment."

Nude, my feet in the cold shallows,
The motion of the water surface
Barely perceptible, and the sand
Of the bottom in fine sharp ridges
Under my toes, I wade out, waist deep
And swim seaward down the narrow inlet.
In the distance, beyond the sand bar,
The combers are breaking, and nearer,
Like a wave crest escaped and frozen,
One white egret guards the harbor mouth.
The immense stellar phenomenon
Of dawn focuses in the egret
And flows out, and focuses in me
And flows infinitely away
To touch the last galactic dust.

This is the prime reality—
Bird and man, the individual
Discriminate, the self evalued
Actual, the operation
Of infinite, ordered potential.
Birds, sand grains, and souls bleed into being;
The past reclaims its own, "I should have,
I could have—It might have been different—"
Sunsets on Saturn, desert roses,
Corruptions of the will, quality—
The determinable future, fall
Into quantity, into the
Irreparable past, history's
Cruel irresponsibility.

This is the minimum negative
Condition, the "Condition humaine,"
The tragic loss of value into
Barren novelty, the condition
Of salvation; out of this alone
The person emerges as complete
Responsible act—this lost
And that conserved—the appalling
Decision of the verb "to be."
Men drop dead in the ancient rubbish
Of the Acropolis, scholars fall
Into self-dug graves, Jews are smashed
Like heroic vermin in the Polish winter.
This is my fault, the horrible term
Of weakness, evasion, indulgence,
The total of my petty fault—
No other man's.

                    And out of this
Shall I reclaim beauty, peace of soul,
The perfect gift of self-sacrifice,
Myself as act, as immortal person?

I walk back along the sandspit,
The horizon cuts the moon in half,
And far out at sea a path of light,
Violent and brilliant, reflected
From high stratus clouds and then again
On the moving sea, the invisible
Sunrise spreads its light before the moon.

My wife has been swimming in the breakers,
She comes up the beach to meet me, nude,
Sparkling with water, singing high and clear
Against the surf. The sun crosses
The hills and fills her hair, as it lights
The moon and glorifies the sea
And deep in the empty mountains melts
The snow of Winter and the glaciers
Of ten thousand thousand years.

THE DRAGON AND
THE UNICORN
(1944–1950)

For
Marthe

εἰμὶ δ' ἐγὼ τὰ μὲν ἄλλα φαῦλος
καὶ ἄχρηστος, τοῦτο δέ μοί πως ἐκ
θεοῦ δέδοται, ταχὺ οἵῳ τ' εἶναι γνῶναι
ἐρῶντά τε καὶ ἐρώμενον. Σώκρατες.

Socrates, in the Lysis

THE DRAGON AND THE UNICORN

I

"And what is love?" said Pilate,
And washed his hands.

     All night long
The white snow falls on the white
Peaks through the quiet darkness.
The overland express train
Drives through the night, through the snow.
In the morning the land slopes
To the Atlantic, the sky
Is thicker, Spring stirs, smelling
Like old wet wood, new life speaks
In pale green fringes of marsh
Marigolds on the edges
Of the mountain snow drifts. Spring
Is only a faint green haze
On the high plains, only haze
And the fences that disappear
Over the horizon, and the
Rails, and the telegraph
Poles and the pale singing wires
Going on and on forever.

All things are made new by fire.
The plow in the furrow, Burns
Or Buddha, the first call to
Vocation, the severed worms,
The shattered mouse nest, the seed
Dripping from the bloody sword.
The sleepers chuckle under
The wheels, mocking the heartbeat.

We think of time as serial
And atomic, the expression
By mechanical means of a
Philosophical notion,
Regular divisibility
With a least common divisor
Of motion by motion, so
Many ticks to a century.
Such a thing does not exist.
Actually, the concept
Of time arose from the weaving
Together of the great organic
Cycles of the universe,
Sunrise and sunset, the moon
Waxing and waning, the changing
Stars and seasons, the climbing
And declining sun in heaven,
The round of sowing and harvest,
And the life and death of man.

The doom of versifying—
Orpheus was torn to pieces
By the vindictiveness of
Women or struck down by the
Jealousy of heaven.

The doom of the testicles—
Chiron's masculinity
Was so intense that all his
Children were adopted and
Later destroyed by the gods.

The deed done, Orestes draws
His steel penis like a snake
From its hole. The sun and moon
In Capricorn, Electra,
The little she goat, bleats and squirms,
Her brother between her thighs.
From whose wounds pour forth both blood

And water, the wine of whose
Maidenhead turns to water
Of baptism, the fiery
Mixture of being and not being.
The artist is his own mother.

Chicago, the train plunges through
A vast dome of electric gloom.
Cold wind, deepening dark, miles
Of railroad lights, 22nd
And Wentworth. The old Chinese
Restaurants now tourist joints.
Gooey Sam where we once roared
And taught the waiters to say
Fellow Worker, is now plush.
As the dark deepens I walk
Out Wentworth, grit under my feet.
The smell of frying potatoes
Seeps through the dirty windows.
The old red light district is
Mostly torn down, vacant lots
Line the railroad tracks. I know
What Marvell meant by desarts
Of vast eternitie. Man
Gets daily sicker and his
Ugliness knots his bowels.
On the sight of several
Splendid historical brothels
Stands the production plant of
Time-Luce Incorporated.
Die Ausrottung der Besten.

Do not cut a hole in the
Side of a boat to mark the
Place where your sword dropped and sank.

In experience each present
Time includes its past and as the
Future appears it is included

In it. Only when we come to
Compare the time of one group of
Facts with another do we have
To imagine a common factor,
The instant. As one time is
Measured against the other, both
Are considered to lie in a
Neutral medium of serial
Instants, or against a linear
Background of dots in series.
With hardly any exceptions
The great philosophers have held
That this kind of time is unreal.

Women of easy virtue,
Nanda and Syata, came
To Buddha before the first
Enlightenment. Ambipali,
A whore richer than princes,
Before the last Nirvana.
Jesus was born in Rachel's tomb,
John's Salome his midwife.

A freshman theme, "It is the
Contention of this paper
That the contemporary world
Is fundamentally corrupt."

The logical positivist,
The savage with an alarm clock,
"It seems to me that human
Spiritual evolution
Progresses from a maximum
To a minimum of
Imagination. It seems
That the pattern of history
Leads man from fantasy to
Reason, from a mythical
To a logical condition.

Perhaps progress consists in
Getting rid of that over
Whelming power of fantasy
Which seems to dominate children
And primitive peoples."

The greatest dragon painter
Who ever lived was Ssu Ma
Tsien. Awesome, terrifying,
His dragons left spectators
Weak and giddy for hours.
When they were shown to the Son
Of Heaven, he had to take
To his bed and thunderstorms
Drenched the Five Regions. The real
Dragons were very flattered.
The Dragon Court decided
That in fact they weren't quite so
Frightening; and as a mark
Of favor the Dragon King
Appeared before Ssu Ma Tsien
As a model for future
Dragons. The painter became
Unconscious with terror and
Never again was able to
Paint dragons because of his
Continuous shuddering.

"The progress of science is
A transition to new and
Better information. Often
The old must be discarded
As false and inadequate.
Philosophy progresses by
Deepening and enriching the
Understanding of principles
Already known. Philosophy
Which discards the past is suspect.
Art, however, does not progress."

Clear after a three day storm,
Phosphorescence in the sea
Off Ireland, the air tropical,
The pole stars high in the sky.
The sun enters the second
Moon of Spring. The hawk turns to
A dove. Hoar frost becomes dew.
The next day, Easter, nineteen
Forty-nine, from Fastenet
All along the coast the bells
Ringing in the birth of the
Irish Republic. Easter
Night, the odor of land off
Holyhead, the special smell
Of Wales, of herbs and turf smoke.

"The human soul is infinitely
Richer than it is aware of.
Its being is so broad and deep
That it can never wholly
Develop and comprehend
Itself in the consciousness.
Man is a mystery to
Himself, a riddle which will
Never be solved in consciousness,
For, should he ever attain to
The internal intuition
Of his whole being he would
Be swallowed up and consumed
In himself." So Leibnitz says.

The great black pseudo classical
Victorian public buildings
Of Liverpool, bombed-out shells,
Everybody too busy
To fix them up. So Rome died,
They were always going to
Get at the ruins next year.
Coal smoke and Spring move down the
Brick-lined gas-lit streets on the

Chill wind from the Mersey.
The Youth Hostel recommends
"A Jew bloke, decent chap, yu knaow,
Runs a plice called Troicycle Ouse."
Friendly as a six months pup,
Enthusiast for the adult
Tricycle, bronzed from tricycling
Over England. It is Pesach,
An austerity Passover,
With matzoth and fish and chips.

Christ blessed the cup with the Kadusha
Sabbath prayer over the wine.
Malkuth, the embodied Glory—
The Mother of God was a
Temple prostitute deflowered
By a chance passerby, or
The Virgin of the Ages—
Essentially the same thing.

I visit the neogothic
Cathedral, almost as handsome
As Sacré-Coeur, the window
Of Gordon bringing opium
And Christ to the Chinese is still
In storage since the war. Down
The hill to Chinatown, sleepy
In Spring sunlight, I eat lunch with
Two Lancashire and two Welsh whores—
Ham and greens, pork tripe and pea pods,
The best meal I'll get in England.
To me, fresh from the States, the girls
Look awfully poor. I will learn
More cosmopolitan standards.
They are full of songs, dirty jokes,
And wisecracks, say, "Yu knaow" every
Third word, act remarkably
Like French girls and utterly
Unlike the bitter London drabs.
Lancashire, if you forget

It is supposed to be English,
Is a musical language
Something like Irish and Welsh.
One of the Lancashire girls
Is a long-legged blonde with
Very knowing eyes, named Clarice.
I spend the night with her and
In the morning she makes breakfast
With two eggs apiece, takes me
Back to bed again for a long
Farewell embrace, then takes me
To the station and helps me
To get my baggage sorted,
Some in a rucksack, the rest
Off to London. I change clothes
In the baggage room, she tips
The baggage clerk, and we do it
One last time amongst the dark
Piles of trunks and suitcases.
She weeps as she sees me off
On the bus to Chester and
Refuses to take any money.
It hasn't taken me long
To find the only place where
I will find friends in Europe.

As the Philosopher says,
"Love is the desire to be
United to the beloved,
To be transported out of
Oneself into the beloved.
So love prefers the least contact
To the greatest distant joy."

Just as the time of mathematics
Is a convention of measure,
So past, present, and future
Are qualifications of
Knowledge. They have no being

102

Outside the experience
Of possible and consequent.
They are the way discursive
Knowledge comes to us, and their
Essential relation is
One of inclusion. The past
Is less experience than the
Present and it than the future.

The tremendous exaltation
Of North Wales glowing with Spring—
Birds and wild flowers everywhere,
Too many to name, the rock walls
And high hedges and sunken fields
Covered with violets and bluebells,
Daffodils at the woods' edges,
Black Welsh cattle and chubby sheep.
Topping the hills above Conway
The Snowdon mountains rise through the
Clouds, unmistakable Tryfan
Dramatic as the great peaks of
Caucasus and Himalaya,
Faint purple aslant the sun with
Blue snow patches, Conway castle
Mellow lavender stone in the
Early evening. Llanrwst,
Capel-Curig, Bettys y Coed,
Idwal Cottage, Llanberis,
Beddgelert, all the beautiful
Names, and the dark blue-eyed people
With their musical voices.
I walk at night through thick forest
Spotted with light by the half moon.
Owls cry all about me, and off
In a nearby meadow, in a cloud
Of moonlight, the grate of a
Corncrake. Suddenly the wood gives
Way to an orchard, nightingales
In the midst of blooming pear trees.

Yang Kuei-fei was hanged on a
Pear tree, and a black bird flew
Away with her bloodstained veil.
Augustine hung his childhood
In a pear tree. In our day
Psychoanalysts decided
It was somebody's penis
And not a pear tree at all.

Climbing Tryfan and the Glyders
With a young telephone lineman,
The rock greasy in driving mist.
The mountains show themselves
A few seconds at a time
But from Tryfan for a quarter
Hour, the sea and islands,
All the purple peaks of Wales
Mottled with soft white clouds,
To the east a brilliant rainbow.

Light is the aptitude of
A point to generate a
Sphere of graded intensity
Indefinitely large.
As the Philosopher says,
"The noblest way to possess
A thing is to possess it
In an immaterial
Manner, that is, possessing
Its form without its matter.
This is the definition
Of knowledge." The dragon
And the unicorn, earth and air.

Pont Aberglaslyn in whirling
Mist like a Chinese painting.
Down to the sea at Port Madoc,
I swim in the cold water.
Pwllheli and Aberdaron
In stiff wind, the busses filled

With plump farm women with baskets.
No one speaks English, everyone
Has that odor of herbs and turf,
The strange gnome-like smell of Wales.
At Aberdaron no boat to
Bardsey, too stiff a wind, so
I loaf four days in a place
Where man is still good, tight grey
Houses, the hedges filled with
Flowers and the sky with birds,
Even the sheep look clean and
Intelligent. The girls have
Plump bright cheeks, deep eyes, and round
Bottoms. In the evening talking
On the old bridge below the
Watermill they sound like thrushes.

If we think of time as really
An aspect of experience
It is easy to realize
That its serial character
Is that of inclusion series,
Like Chinese boxes or the tubes
Of a telescope, and the time
Of the mathematician is
Simply the surface along which
The elements of experience
Fit into each other. Each
Person's experience grows
From an insignificant
Indivisible atom to
An infinite universe.
Each simpler experiential
Level telescopes into
The more complex as we look back
And analyze experience
And see it as consequential.
We call this time and the simpler
We attribute to the past and
Imagine a still more complex

In the future. Actually,
Of course, no one has ever
Seen either the past or the
Future, we live in the present.

No sign of the wind letting up,
So I leave Brenda Chamberlain
To her island of ten thousand birds
And go on to Dolgelley and climb
Cader Idris in the evening
And sleep on top in a mist
Like cotton wool so dense I can't
See my primus stove when I stand
In the dark. My flashlight shines
Against mist like a plaster wall.
After midnight the sky clears
And the soft Summer stars move
Over me from England to the sea.

The heart's mirror hangs in the void.
Vision blossoms in the night
Like stars opening in the brain.
Jehovah created the world
In six days. The Bible does not
Mention the nights. He holds the
Creation of the night in
Concealment for His own ends.
There is no reality
Except that of experience
And experience is the
Conversation of persons.

The next day, up the river
Through the hills, through Llangadfyn
And the high moors of the Border.
I stop in a fisherman's inn
Just this side Welshpool. Cold mutton
And black beer for supper. The guests
Are English, decent people, but
Too much like drawings in *Punch*.

I go into the pub, full of
Peasants singing and drinking beer.
No one speaks English except
To me, but they are all very
Friendly and buy me drinks and
Ask wistfully if I think
America plans to go to war.
Not having been in the habit
Of using "we" when I mean the
State Department, it takes time
To explain that America
Is several different persons,
Some of them like Welsh peasants.
They are curious about John
L. Lewis, who is to Wales what
Giannini is to Italy.
The room reeks very pleasantly
Of the Welsh smell. I shall never
Know what it is, you can't ask,
"I say, what makes you smell so odd?"
Later when I tried to get some
Information on the subject
From Dylan Thomas, he was quite
Put out. But my hiking guides,
Shropshire and the Border, North Wales,
Still smell in California.
In the morning, loud with birds,
Wales drops behind me. Never
Will I find better people
Or a more beautiful country.

All things, all entities of
Whatsoever nature are
Only perspectives on persons.
Each moment of the universe
Is a moment of choice, chosen
Out of the infinite system
Of possibility which forms
The content of experience,
The continuously shifting

And flowing organism
Of relationships, its form
Determined by the character
Of the willing agent, its
Contents the evaluative
Strands and strains, the perspectives
Connecting with all other persons.
Each moment of the universe
And all the universes
Are reflected in each other
And in all their parts and
Thence again in themselves.
It is simpler to see this
As a concourse of persons, all
Reflecting and self-reflecting
And the reflections and the
Reflective medium reflecting.

Sunday, Shrewsbury and crowds
Boating on the Severn. Back and
Forth and up and down Shropshire
Through the entranced landscape.
Always before I had thought
Housman a conventional
Sort of Theocritan, Versailles
Peasant kind of poet, but it
Is all just as he says. Broom,
Hawthorn, cherry, the wind on
Wenlock Edge, the Clun villages
Drowsing away the centuries,
Clee Beacon above Ludlow and
The bell in the pure tower
Of St. Lawrence scattering
The quarters over the town.
No redcoats marching to drums,
No hangings at the moment—
He neglected to mention
The haunting color of the glass
In St. Lawrence, like the blue eyes
Of Welsh queens. Hiking along

The road by Onwy, a young
Veterinarian gives me a ride.
He is leaving for London
And America next week
And taking a last drive over
Shropshire, so I see it all again,
From Shrewsbury to Leominster,
From Much Wenlock to Montgomery.
He is a remarkably
Civilized young man with few
Of the appetites of commerce,
But he says of Wenlock Edge,
"Chap wrote a poem about it,
Couldn't make head or tail of it."
Oh well, it's all there and
He could see it, anyway.
After supper we walk in
The park at Ludford above
The town and the castle hazy
With evening fires, with Clee
Beacon in the distance on the
Long swell of hill above the
Tower of St. Lawrence, all paling
And then gone in the darkness.
We bid farewell and promise
To look each other up. Poor
Bastard, he doesn't know what is
Going to happen to him, he's
To teach at Pullman, Washington.

Every item of this cosmos
Of possibilities is the
Mode by which I apprehend
A person. Each person chooses
His own time and space as he
Continuously adjusts
Himself to other persons
With whom he is in closest
Contact. They of course may appear
Not only as persons. For the

Moment an onrushing train
Seems more important than a
Distant wife or dead mother.
South to Hereford, swinging a
Sticks of Housman's cherry cut
On Wenlock Edge, a great red
Lion of a Cathedral, and
Across to the Wye, the placid
River winding through meadows,
Orchards, and forests, the apples
All in bloom over red and white
Hereford cattle, the people
Friendly and open, bright and clear—
Westerners. A wind comes up
In the afternoon and the boats
Of fishermen revolve on the
River. St. Briavel's high on the
Hills above the river, the road
Climbing through apple orchards full
Of nightingales, past stone-troughed,
Terraced fish ponds, like the aging
Cassiodorus built himself,
"Pleasant is the glittering
Of the sun today on these
Banks because it flickers so,"
Tired of the court of the Goth
And the empty-headed Senate,
In the last ruin of the world
In Squillace, fourteen hundred
Years ago.

St. Briavel's Hostel,
A purple ruined castle,
The gate house and some of the front
Repaired and rebuilt, the rest
Tapering off gently into
Rubble. The inhabitants
Completely improbable.
Two youths, not together, who

Have both read my poetry.
A steel spectacled, balding
Australian social science
Teacher, "educator" he
Called himself, full of the most
Arrant nonsense about both
Baden-Powell and Wilhelm Reich—
The B-P Spirit and Free Love
For Infants, a combination
He explained dialectically
(As Hilary Belloc says,
It must be frightful to live
Where you have to travel ten
Days to meet somebody who
Doesn't dot his capital I's.)
A precocity of ten
With a mother who looked like
Something by Gutzon Borglum,
Who knew literally everything.
She thought Petrie better than Breasted,
The body of Montezuma a fake,
Disapproved of Schliemann,
Thought Picasso was declining,
Stalin would have more trouble with
Tito than he had with Trotsky,
Simone de Beauvoir wrote atrociously,
Genet was an American fad,
The planet Pluto was smaller
Than estimated, Einstein
Did not compare with Clerk Maxwell,
Joe Lewis was unbeatable,
The greatest strain in racing
History was Man o' War's.
The curious thing about all
These opinions is their soundness.
By the fire, playing a game
Involving the guessing and
Plotting of quadratic curves,
The child says, "Mother dear, I find

This random talk excessively
Distracting." They're from Cambridge,
Castle-crawling this trip, did
Cathedrals last year, mountains next.

Morning, down through the river
Meadows and the Forest of Deane,
The last taste of King Arthur's world,
To Tintern Abbey, rooks wheeling
In the crystal sky through pure
Gothic planes and spaces as I
Eat lunch from red sandstone purple
With time. The vast muddy Severn,
Bristol vast and busy but still
About St. Mary Redcliffe
With the hushed voice of an age
Founded on contemplation.

States like men are born in blood,
Die first in the heart and head.

The history of choice which
The person traces through his
Chiliacosm, through all the
Possible universes of
All his possibilities, like
A worm track through cheese, is what
Has been called the empiric
Ego—the self of Buddhist and
Similar polemic. It has,
Obviously, no existence
Except as the perspective
On shifting perspectives.

Bath a stageset for Terence,
One of the world's unlikely
Cities, as freakish as Venice.
In the midst of the colonnades
And the swarming well-fed people,
Bath Abbey, immense and absurd,

Like the skeleton of a
Whale or a dirigible,
Built by Walpole Gothicizing,
The most eighteenth century
Product of the Middle Ages.

All the possibilities of
Any instant and of any
Series of instants are both
Unlimited, but they are
Only the possibilities
Organized and structured by those
Specific situations, the
Possibilities of just those
Consequences and no others.

The close of Wells Cathedral
Gold and green in the afternoon,
Inside, the combination
Of Protestant destruction
And British worship of the dead
Is beginning to pall on me.
Glastonbury at twilight,
The Tor over the hollow land,
The Graal procession and the court
Of the Fisher King behind the mist,
The black-robed queens and the dead
Arthur in a barge on the river.

But consequence is only
Possibility seen backwards,
So the manifold which garbs
The person and which he thinks
Of as himself and as all the
Content of his experience—
The universe—all he has done,
Knows, plans, or hopes, all his ideas
And sensations, however
Delusional or illusory—
Is his responsibility.

We each choose in all its details
The exact world we live in.
Do you complain of war, famine,
Pestilence, treason, and murder?
They exist because you choose them.
They are the consequences
Of the movements of your will.

Night in Somerset alone
Under the windy stars, an inn
Where the host kept me till midnight
Talking of Amuriky in
The soft speech of Somerset,
Like Quaker talk without their pride.
Exeter half in ruins,
The cathedral shored up and closed.
Cornwall like tepid barley water.

Over the hills and fields to
Derek Savage's thatched clay
Cottage in a narrow moist
Valley by a ruined mill.
Three days of hospitality
And passionate talk. How good
To meet someone in this world
With his own convictions and
Careless of gossip and fashion.
The only young English poet
Of working class extraction—
Barker is Irish, Thomas, Welsh—
But certainly by far the most
Distinguished both in appearance
And opinions. Connie
Savage an educated Kate Blake.

"One morning as I was sitting
By the fire, a great cloud came
Over me, and a temptation
Beset me; but I sat still.

And it was said, 'All things come
By nature,' and the elements
And the stars came over me,
So that I was in a manner
Quite clouded with it. But as
I sat still under it and
Let it alone, a living
Hope arose in me, and a true
Voice which said, 'There is a living
God who made all things.' Instantly
The cloud and the temptation
Vanished away, and life rose
Over it all; my heart was glad,
And I praised the living God."

"They betray the Truth," says Derek,
Sitting amongst his children.
No answer to Pilate's question.

High above Yarcombe the wind
Dies at sunset and I rest
In a hanging meadow. The land
Falls away for long blue miles
Down the trough of glacial valley.
In the deep resonant twilight
The stars open like wet flowers.
Young rabbits play on the hummocks
And vanish as a white owl comes
Cruising low over the ground.
He lights on a post and inspects
Me with curious owl-like quirks.
I go on in the starlight.
Lights of farms and villages
On the high ridges reflect
The constellations. Down
The hill in the soft thick night
The nightingales are singing, bird
After bird, for mile on mile.

George Fox was a bloody man,
A ranter who went naked.
Out of his violent heart
Peace poured through his skin like dream,
Like a moonlight around him.

Finnan haddie and tomatoes
For late supper in Yarcombe Inn.
Next day, a Thomas Hardy wind.
Crimson orchids in the hedgerows.
Salisbury Cathedral
A form at least as pure as
Chartres, like a stone waterfall
Descending or a fountain
Of stone ascending to heaven.
Inside, the hideous British
Necrophilia and the rancid
Stink of the Church of England.

I am walking westward along
The road across Salisbury
Plain in the great wind of the place,
Like a trade wind; and my mind is
Full of the climbing silver grey
Cascade of the cathedral spire.
All around me larks are throwing
Themselves frantic into heaven.
The air is shivering with the
Singing of a thousand larks.
Closer to earth there are hoopoes
With their lunging flight and their strange
Desolate crying; and dashing
Away from my walking, great hares
And moorhens. All at once I come
Around a copse and see the road
Stretching away to the west, white
In the glare of late afternoon,
And beside it, purple, immense
With shadow, Stonehenge, lonelier
Than ten thousand years.

116

Alone, deep in contemplation
An hour, and then a little yellow
Man in chambray shorts and jumper
Pops up and asks, "Excuse, please,
Is possible could be natural
Phenomenon?" He turns out
To be a Karen, studying
To be a pilot at the airfield
Nearby, with all the jungle's
Note-taking greed for Western
Learning and science. Another
Logical positivist
"All things come by nature." On the
Way back, lovers walking, arm in
Arm, out of Amesbury, towards
The sunset and the ancient stone.

All the past is not apparent
In most presents, certainly not
Those of high or complex order,
But neither is all the space of
The foreground apparent between
Parallel lines as they recede.
Of course the past is all there, it
Is simply not all relevant.

Coming up the hill looking back
Over Winchester, the looping
River and the vast cathedral—
Thin fog with sun breaking through—
Two aged men in an ancient
Churchyard cleaning the gravestones
Under a calling cuckoo.

England is gone and London,
Sicker than New York, takes its place.

The spider monkeys revolve
Over their island with ghostly
Jollification. A rhesus

Masturbates, observing
Himself in a hand mirror.
Death and taxes, the affairs
Of gods and men, go their way.
And Hseuh-fung said that
Even these inconsequential
Creatures carry the Buddha
Mirror in their hearts. Kew Gardens,
Beyond Lebanon's cedars,
Sequoias from California,
Poor and spindly in the smoke
And lifeless London sunlight.

Tense tiger-eyed women who take
My lack of inhibitions for
An invitation to the games
Of scatological children.
The editor of . . . ., his
Power gone, being treated
Like a nigger by drunken
Cryptostalinist fairies.
The Chelsea set being refined,
Which means insulting each other
In sundry complicated ways.
The London Anarchist Group
Like a debating club at an
Exclusive Kansas private school.
Emma Goldman said, years ago,
"You're not British anarchists,
You're just British." A blonde barrage
Balloon, the power behind
. . . ., a frantic
Imitation of Mary
McCarthy, Rita Hayworth,
And Simone de Beauvoir Sartre.
. . .'s hideous caddy
Bubbling like a poisoned pudding.
Intellectual parties,
Orgies of foolish snobbery,
Bad manners, and illiteracy.

The Irish are not considered
Human, the Scotch and Welsh subject
To worse chauvinism than
Can be found in the Deep South.
Everywhere, hate, covetousness,
And envy of money-grubbing
Americans. More talk of
Money than I have ever heard.
However, my pension is
A haven of old ladies,
Coal smoke, and cat piss, presided
Over by a retired colonel
Who eats breakfast in morning clothes.
"When I was military
Advisor to the Sultan of
Abadabad, we knew how
To handle fellows like Pollitt,
Gave them a whiff of grape, that
Quieted them, no more trouble."
I thought whiffs of grape were given
Only in Henty's boys' books.
The last total male in London.

Walking through Soho on Greek Street,
One of the soiled drabs who are the
Special fauna of the place comes
Up and says, as they all do,
With exquisite English tact,
"Come along." I say, "How much?"
She says, "Thirty shilling." I say,
"What've you got worth thirty shilling?"
She says, "Ow, if you wants them
Circus tricks they's French girls over
On Romilly Street 'll oblige
You for a pound." I say, "Thank you."
As I cross Romilly Street
A girl comes towards me, tall, heavy
Black hair like a Mexican girl,
Exophthalmic, dark blue-grey eyes,
Full hips and the heavy breasts of

Provence, narrow waist, spectacular
Legs on skyscraper heels. She says,
"Allô?" I say, "Que fais?"
She says, "Vous parlez français?"
I say, "Un petit peu." She
Speaks hardly any English.
I explain that I have
A very special rendezvous
But I will come back at eight
And we can go to dinner.
She says, "Vous me trouverez ici
Tout le temps, si je ne travaille pas
Dans ma chambre. Restez ici."
We go to the Club Suisse and then
To the Gargoyle. We become fast
Friends and I introduce her to
All the right people as an
Existentialiste. She tells me that
She was the lover of a French
Communist who turned out to be
A finger man for the Nazi
Extermination squads, so she
Can never go back to Paris.
This seems to me a good record
To run for office on in
Present-day Paris, but she
Is definite and expressive
About what would happen to her.
She is a Nizarde, "Nini" for
Andrée, (I thought Nini was Jeanne),
Certainly the most impressive
Woman to enter a room with
I have ever known and one of
The very best lays. She tells me
She is a sadist "seulement
Pour le commerce." But as the nights
Go on she gets quite rough and I
Spend the days in a tingle.
"Les Anglais sont bêtes, saints,
Et pervers." "Et lourds et plausibles."

"Oui, oui, oui, très plausibles!"
The night before I leave London
I give her two boxes of nylons
Which I had brought for a Chelsea
Writress who turned out to be
Too refined for nylons. They are
Opera length and deep brownish black.
She is enraptured and takes
Off all her clothes and puts them on.
For a while she struts before me
Making French noises of approval,
And then suddenly turns and butts
My shoulder and weeps violently,
"Ah, le monde est méchant, mon
Petit, le monde est très méchant."

It is doubtful if the world
Presents itself in any
Important aspects under
The forms of serial time
And atomic space. It is
True that the intellect has
Come to be conditioned by them,
But important experience
Comes to us in freedom and
Is realized as value,
And the intellect alone
Can know nothing of freedom
And value because it is
Concerned with the necessary
And they are by definition
Unnecessitated. Love
Of course is the ultimate
Mode of free evaluation.
Perfect love casts out knowledge.

The *Daily Mail*, "We view with some
Amusement the naïveté
Of the Italians, who are
Permitting themselves to be

Chivvied by the Americans
Into a most unwise over-
Expanded hydroelectric
Development. The French are
To be commended for having
Resisted and continuing
To resist similar coaxing
From the new 'bosses' of Europe.
With true Gallic sagacity,
They cling to well-known facts,
And show no desire to substitute
Electricity derived from
Coal for the inferior
Product derived from water."

The dragon and the unicorn.

II

The Art of Worldly Wisdom
Comes to me by air across
The continent and over
The Atlantic. I get a beer
And cut open the package
On the Place de l'Opéra,
Hideous and jangling with
The Sahibs of the Plan Marshall
And their nasty virgin daughters.
Poems twenty-five years old—
All that old agony and
Wonder strikes me in the face
In the glare of downtown Paris,
The bankrupt faubourg of hatreds
And Bonapartes. I take the bus
To the Closerie des Lilas
And sit on the leafy terrace
Looking at the book in amazement.

Was it all true once? Just like
It says? I cannot find the past.
It is only anecdotes
For company and the parching
Of a few more hidden nerves
Each year.

        I get up and go
To dinner to the room of my
Only friend on this continent,
A blonde Bretonne servant girl
Who earns forty francs an hour
(Three-fifty to the dollar).
Her little boy has TB
And impetigo and doesn't
Even own a ball except one
He ingeniously made of rags.
She has just lost her job, but
We have potage Parmentier,
Salade, haricots verts, cheval,
And pommes with fines herbes and black
Coffee fresh roasted and ground
For each cup, and cerises
Which she has managed to chill
By some occult process. I bring
Some Pelure d'oignon. We sit
In the great heat of the long
Drought of nineteen forty-nine
And eat cherries and discuss
The papers which must be signed
So the boy can go to a
Sanatorium in the Pyrenees,
The hirondelles like angels
Of St. Michael over the roofs.
Suddenly into the court
Of this slum, under the beams
Of heat and the crushing sun,
La Vie en rose always on
Somebody's radio, the past

Returns, the youth, the agony,
And the vertigo and the love
That always failed or broke or turned
Away. And with the past and its
Bound loyalty and love, comes,
I suppose, the art of worldly
Wisdom as guest to this feast
Of horse meat and fugitive
Loyalty and passing faith.

We put Christian to sleep and go
To the Gaîté Montparnasse,
La Lune dans le fleuve jaune. Irish
Plays are all the rage this season.
After it is over I ask
Léontine what she thinks of it.
"Comme ci—comme ça, one revolution
Is much like another."

Said Pilate, "What are facts? Don't
Talk to me about facts, I
Am fact." Who can escape from
The shadow of his own head?

Cornemuse, musette, and vielle,
Full of calvados and poiré,
We dance Gaelic flings older than Rome,
On the Rue Vercingétorix.

The first real Fourteenth since the war,
Yvonne and I lie on the quai
Watching the illuminations.
The years pass, the Summers go,
And our few days fall away
From us like the falling stars;
But that glory of rockets,
Showered on sky and river,
On our nightbound eyes and lips,
Will always last. That is what
"Always" means, and all it means.

So each creates his own world,
Polar and antipolar,
Medium, end, and result
Of the act of will, falling
Sparkling through the void, spools of
Good and evil turned on the
Seven-bladed lathe of heaven.

Raindrops spatter the Marne with
Quick discs, a rainbow appears
Over the handsome nineteenth
Century Château Ménier
(Now deserted by debased taste
For a functionalist villa).
The young wheat, just turning gold,
Grows close against the marble walls.
A broken stream trickles through
Wrecked bear pens and aviaries.
We make love in the deep bed
Of the little forest while
Birds cry in the rain over us.

Many women have said goodbye
To me and someday we will say
Goodbye also. At last the hands
Unbraid themselves and the head turns
Away taking the eyes and lips
Away finally forever.
The cords of the heart that were so
Tightly knotted are untied.

Gauguin's last picture—what word
In the final panting fever
In Tahiti? Brittany—
Sunless Winter evening,
Snow, grey sky, not a flush
Of color, blackish brown buildings,
No orange, no green, no red anymore.

Jacqui doesn't believe in
Wasting time. In the dancing
She keeps saying, "Quand faisons-nous
Une poudre? Votre ami, il trouve
Le jitterbug meilleur que l'amour."
At last he and Carmen get
A surfeit of Antillais jazz
And we go to a hotel.
Just before dawn Jacqui uses
The bidet and then leans out
On the balcony, with her
Lovely bottom reared against
The warm empty night above
The tracks of the Gare du Nord,
And says, "Les étoiles, les étoiles
Reculantes, elles s'éloignent
De nous. How you say étoiles
En anglais?" Did she read that
In a book? If so, what book?

The mechanical constructs of
Space-time are by definition
Not accessible to the will.
That is why they were invented.
Choice is only between persons.
The will is the instrument
Of interpersonal concourse.

Late night, walking from La Villette
All the way to Montparnasse—
As I come near the river,
Fog gathers around the lights,
And the whores swim in and out
Of the dark like drowned women.
Crossing the Isle St. Louis,
Where Restif carved his memoirs,
And time has forgot itself,
Out of a high window floats
A girl's voice—Guillaume Machaut—

"Douce dâme"—with its heart-
Breaking cadence on the word
"Seulement," and that is all—
The black river and the fog
Glowing faintly in the light
Of a waning quarter moon.

When one act of will is compared
With another, when it is
Necessary to find a
Neutral component of all
Possibilities, the unit
By which to measure potencies,
Space-time is invented, but it
Is no more real in an absolute
Sense than the ruler is part of
The cloth which the tailor measures.

August . . . south through stubble fields
To the South and Italy.
The middle age of Summer.
Light and shadow both lie long
On the haystacks and poplars.
The world's most hideous
Suburban villas pass by us
In a series of discreet winces.
The narrow level fields of
The Isle de France, looking like
Indiana, the dusty forests.
Orléans and the Loire, at once
The tensions of the narrow
Gutted North relax.
Pompadour in her portraits
By Boucher and Fragonard,
The heads on the bodies of
Stone sphinxes, France at her best,
The best years of her best king—
The thought of the thinking flesh.

Blois and François' folly, that
Damned staircase that looks as though
It was about to fall down.
Incredible that it has stood
So long. "The Thirteenth, greatest
Of centuries," it's possible.
St. Nicolas, buffeted
By the centuries, but still
Nobler than the vanity
Of even the best monarch.

Dinner in a peasant auberge,
Everybody inspects the
Vélos. "De Paris en Italie?
Incroyable! Formidable!"
Grilled pork chops, fried potatoes,
Tomatoes, beans in vinegar,
Fresh cheese, pears, wine, and coffee,
And the magnificent bread
Of Touraine. Just looking at it,
We weep for joy after the
Rancid papier mâché turds
They sell in Paris. We shake
Hands with everybody and
Pedal on down the river,
Wobbling, heavy with food.

We camp on the Loire, the vélos
Parked under a rose bush, the
Sleeping bags under acacias,
And careen down the swift current,
Impossible to stand, much less
Swim against it. Two owls chatter
In the trees as the twilight
Comes, lavender and orange
Over the white reaches of
Water and the whiter sandbars,
And the first starlight dribbling
On the rushing river.

Although the possibilities
Of each instant are infinite
They are the possibilities
Of only that instant, that point
Of triangulation in which
The person places himself
In relation to others. You
Can move only from one point.
This necessitous character
Of consequence is what
Has given rise in the West
To the conception of sin,
In the East to that of Karma.

Chaumont, brilliant in the sun,
The working of a consistent
Principle, the best of the
Big châteaux. Amboise dull and
Hot in August midafternoon,
And then a cool hand, over
The chapel doorway the high
Relief of St. Eustache and
The cruciferous stag, almost
As touching as Pisanello's.

High above the Loire on the way
To the Cher and Chenonceaux—
The Pagode de Choiseul.

ETIENNE FRANÇOIS, DUC DE CHOISEUL,
PENETRE DES TEMOIGNAGES
D'AMITIE, DE BONTE, D'ATTENTION,
DONT IL FUT HONORE PENDANT
SON EXIL PAR UN GRAND NOMBRE
DE PERSONNES EMPRESSEES DE SE
RENDRE EN CES LIEUX, A FAIT
ELEVER CE MONUMENT, POUR
ETERNISER SA RECONNAISSANCE.

1760.

In the center
Of a geometrical
Forêt, his hunting park,
Waiting the patience of the best
Of kings, he and his friends in
Mandarin coats and powdered
Wigs, duchesses and the girls
Of the neighbors in transparent
Trousers, playing chinoiseries
Under the colored lanterns.
Ten petits-scouts and a chef-scout,
Scrambling up the staircases.
The chef-scout looks like Raimu,
Is this the B-P facies?
From the top, all of golden
Touraine in the August glitter.
He outwitted Catherine
And expelled the Jesuits;
Walpole says, "Gallantry without
Delicacy was his constant
Pursuit," a compliment from that
Source. Achilles loafing in Hell
With his harem, Philoxena,
Briseis, Iphigenia,
Helen, and Penthesilea.

It is true that being is
Responsibility, beyond
The speculations of Calvin,
St. Thomas, or Augustine,
Ontology is ethical.

Chenonceaux, the sun low and
Fishermen poling a boat
Under the arches, a boy
Wading up to his arms along-
Side in the weedy water.
Bléré, a foire and carrousel,
All the world drunker than peach
Orchard boars, dashing about

On bicycles. A fine dinner
With lots of the mild local wine,
At the next table a party
Of Anglaises with Rackham daughters,
Quite put about by the foire.
We camp by the Cher in the town,
Till two a.m. an orchestra
Plays beatless renditions of
Le Jazz. As the dawn comes under
The arches of the bridge, the first
Fishermen appear in the
Dewfall.
            Tours dusty, hot and bright.
Above the Loire, defacing
The landscape, a monstrously
Ugly moderne Franciscan church,
Windows like kaleidoscopes,
Rouault goosed up for the masses.
In Tours the streets are named for
The famous of France, of the world,
And of the locality, with
Biographical details
On each street sign, a brave custom.
The cathedral very English,
Shattered by Protestants.
We eat lunch under the chestnuts
In a bring-your-own café.

This terrifying picture
In which you are the cause of
The wars and disasters of
Your history is transcended
By the realization that
They are those possibilities
Which you have chosen to throw
Into sharpest perspective.

All day southward to Poitiers,
Through a world of rivers and
Castles, white shorn wheatfields and

Ripening grapes and suddenly
Tile roofs and cream-colored houses,
The mark of civilization,
Of Rome and the South. Poitiers
An outlyer of Ravenna,
Saint Jean a ruined provincial
San Vitale, Notre Dame
Romanesque with the last
Sense of the Arian mystery
Of the Goths in the narrow
Aisles around the apse. St. Hilaire,
The aisle arches interlaced
In quincunxes Sir Thomas missed.
Here the saintly pagan queen
Fought once more for Julian's
Lost cause and lost it again,
And Sweet William the Lewd, crowned
Poet, the first open flame
From the erotic gnostic fires.

Tant las fotei com auziretz
Cen ce quatre vint et ueit vetz,
Q'a pauc no .i rompei mos corretz
E mos arnes
E no .us puesc dir lo malaveg
Tan gran m'en pres.
Ges no .us sai dir lo malaveg
Tan gran m'en pres.
E.l pans fo blancs e.l vins fo bos
E.l pebr' espes.
                        White bread, good
Wine, and plenty of pepper.

Iam, dulces amico venito—
Dum caupona verterem—
If Hafiz is a mystic,
How many of the poems of
The Carmina Burana
Are at least as mystical?
Radegunde's tower, and the

Memory of Venantius
Fortunatus, that mild
And felicitous heart writing
Odes for gifts of plovers' eggs
And violets, compliments
On new dresses of lady saints,
And just once—exaltation—
Vexilla regis prodeunt
Fulget Crucis mysterium—
The royal banners forward go,
The Cross shines forth with mystic glow.
Radegunde's beauty still quivers
In the pages of Dill and Raby,
And Venantius' hymn still chills
The scalps of millions every
Second Sunday before Easter.

In the archetypal couple
Left is evil and right is good.
In their embrace left lies against
Right and right against left and
Good absorbs and transmutes evil.

Angoulême late at night with
Storm brewing, violent rain
On the steep streets after midnight.
Morning grey and vast over
Angoumois with a lace of lightning
Constantly above the valley
Of the Anguienne to the south.
The rain trickles out with a
High clear wind. The monument
To Carnot on the main Place,
Two female figures, one happy
And inspiring, one seated
And discouraged, (the Laws of
Thermodynamics?).
                    The Rempart
De Beaulieu,

"PAUL VALERY
S'EST ARRETE ICI LE IX
DECEMBRE MDCCCCXXXI
'—O récompense après une pensée
Qu'un long regard sur le calme des dieux!—' "

And immediately beyond—

"EN MDCCCVI LE GENERAL
RESNIER, NE A ANGOULEME
MDCCXXIX—MDCCCXI
S'EST ELANCE DE L'ENDROIT,
TOUR LADENT, EFFECTUANT AINSI
LE PREMIER
VOL SANS MOTEUR AVEC UN
APPAREIL DE SON INVENTION
CONSTRUIT A ANGOULEME."

Through fields, vineyards, and forests,
The two rivers wind away
Below, the mellow civilized
Land stretches on and on southwards.
In the hanging gardens a white
And a colored peacock both
Titivating after rain,
A peahen and two peachicks
Busy catching worms. Down past
Terraced water, like St. Briavel's
And Cassiodorus' ponds,
Fat French goldfish jumping for
Post-rain insects, to the church
Of St. Ausone—canonized—
The old sentimentalist
And sensualist dreaming away
The centuries (the church is
New but the site ancient)
Amongst the chestnuts and peafowl
Waiting for Valéry and
Carnot and Le Général Resnier.
St. Pierre, neat, calm, and splendid,

134

On the façade St. George spitting
A sort of Gila monster,
Certainly one of the really
Great equestrian statues.
Vernet and Abadie dreaming
Of the glory of Langue d'Oc.
Over the hills into the
Dordogne watershed, all the farm
Houses built by Theodoric.
Périgueux—St. Front—Diana
Of Ephesus recumbent
On the fertile flesh of the Midi,
The white interior marked by
Abadie's lucid intellect.
The Arabic cavern of
St. Etienne, the ruins
Of another kind of vision.
The specialities of
Périgord, pâtés truffés,
Monbazillac, and brochet steamed
In wine, copies of the reindeer
On the walls of the restaurant.
In the slums under St. Front
An akimbo hotel full
Of elderly, very drunken
And very affectionate whores
Who try hard to entice us in.
High on the hills across the Isle
Where the Gallic chiefs lived once,
A deserted Theodoric
Farm, the well dry, red sunset
On the white breasts of St. Front.

The vélos plunge through heather
On the steep roads above the
Vézère. Les Eyzies, a good
Place for man to have started
In Europe, a pity he
Ever left. Today the natives
Are surely less civilized

Than the Cro-Magnons. An Auberge de la
Jeunesse Française camp in a cave,
All the jeunesse singing without
Stop, even during dinner,
The adolescent girls very
Unfrench with magnificent
Breasts. What is causing this change
In one generation in this
Country once without a mammal?
We leave for the river bank
And camp there in the evening.
It is easy to see the bison
Grazing in the meadows, smoke
Rising from the caves and huts.
Formidable bread, the best
We will ever find in France.

Deep in the bowels of mystery
Where young Cro-Magnons had their
Foreskins shorn, a wiry little
Peasant woman with a lantern
Says, "Regardez! Le dos! Les cornes!
Regardez! L'oeil! Le nez! La bouche!"
It is sad but true, the greatest
Cave artist was the Abbé Breuil.
On up to Lascaux, which if not
A fake points to lamentable
Taste amongst our protoplasts—
Sid Grauman's Cro-Magnon Theatre.

Every world is the reflection
Of the ones about it. Every
Event must take place in every
World in order. All existence
Is like an endless chain hanging
From infinite heaven and
Gradually drawn up. This world
Of yours seems like the last link,
But this is only an illusion
Of perspective. Within the

136

Atoms of your streaming blood
Millions of Troys burn every
Hour. This is the interest
You have taken in the concourse
Of persons of which you are a part.

Condat, we make camp back of a
Factory by the Vézère
And get dubious water
From a farm. The son is in
Training and runs round and round
The field till after dark. He
And his family are as poor,
As friendly, and as generous
As Neapolitans. We cook
Spaghetti with goat cheese on the
Primus and drink Monbazillac
Chilled from the twilit river.

Through Brive to Tulle, mean and dirty.
Through the mountains, lumbering
Villages, wood smoke in the air,
Old men and knitting women
And children watching the few
Cows and goats, the girls great flirts.
"Out at daybreak goes the farmgirl
With flock and spindle and fresh wool.
In her little herd are a lamb,
A donkey, a calf, and a heifer.
She frowns at the scholar sitting
On the turf, 'What are you doing,
Mister? Come and play with me.' "
You can always tell the
Prosperity of the country
And the value of labor
By who can afford to watch goats.

Argentât, camp in a pasture
On the upper Dordogne, the farm
Of a lean, wise old peasant with

A bustling tiny woman
He carefully lets us know
Is his mistress, not his wife.
Much talk of ordinary life
In the States, as distinguished from
The tourist businessmen they'd seen—
The price of beef, of bread, of clothes,
The financing of a farm,
The government farm programs,
Farm machinery, wages.
In the evening a foire
In Argentât, rather skimpy,
And in the night a thunderstorm
Cannonading the hillsides
And solid masses of rain. My
Himalayan tent leaks for the
First time in its life. Morning,
Broken clouds on the hills, swathes
Of mist on the river, and
Wading in mist to their shoulders,
Or with their heads lost in mist,
Fishermen like Chinese sages.
The French philosophy of
Fishing is at least as
Civilized as their attitude
Toward sex. They expect nothing but
Satisfaction from either.

Down the blue, winding river
Through forested hills to Beaulieu,
A fine portal on the church
And a hostel where the river
Teems with washerwomen,
Swallows, and fishermen.

The moral atom of this world,
The irreducible minimum,
Might be the aspect some person
Assumes to me as a speck
Of dust on the edge of the most

138

Remote imagined galaxy.
This of course is a relation
To myself projected and
Confounded with another.

A Harvest Fête on the local
Liberation Day, dancing
In the streets of Latronquière,
The procession led by a sword,
A flag on a spear, a loaf,
A sheaf king, and a full chalice,
A platter with cooked food—the Graal.
The sacraments of pagan Gaul
Will survive other liberations.

Through the highlands to Figeac,
A smelly town but still the France
Before three ruinous wars.
In the early morning old men
Busy whittling sabots, bakers'
Ovens like those in Pompeii,
Blacksmiths forging coulters, just
Like in Chaucer, cartwrights with
Spokeshaves at work on creamy
Sweet-smelling wood of new wagons.
The aubergiste is enchanted
To see me again, and produces
An excellent dinner and
In the morning, "un breakfast"
With scrambled eggs. Incroyable.

Rodez, back in civilization
After the Cantal, the cathedral
A red animal like Hereford,
And looted, too, like England.
Pound's wind blowing west through Langue d'Oc.

All day through the gorges and hills,
We get to Albi late at night,
A fine emergency repast

At our commercial hotel,
Bouillon, cassoulet with boiled beef,
Haricots verts with pommes, cold with
Oil and vinegar like Italy,
Wine as heavy as Burgundy,
Slabs of spongy white cheese, and great
Heaps of fruit, coffee, and anisette.
Then we walk slowly through the
Clear starlight to Sainte Cécile.

The stars over Sainte Cécile,
The five stars and the wide dark space,
Deneb and the cross of heaven,
The swan of Leda, black now,
His work done, and jewelled,
And climbing into his heart the
Vast uprushing, mountainous thought.
Beyond under the Pole Star,
The évêché silhouetted
Pale against the deep sky and
Stabbed with cross lights from the high
Windows of the ancient houses,
And from the highest, like a square
Cut topaz, a phonograph
Spilling *La Vie en rose*,
And inside the évêché
The rests of twisted Lautrec,
Lines like shrivelled mountain pines.

Ultimately the fulfillment
Of reality demands that
Each person in the universe
Realize every one of the
Others in the fullness of love.

Every day we eat ourselves
Drowsy in our little hotel
On the Vigan and sleep with
The rustle of the massive
Chestnut trees in our ears and

The warble of two small but
Softly musical fountains.
One of the chestnuts, blasted
In this year's historic drought,
Has just put forth new pale green stars
Of leaves and delicate tiers
Of unreal blossoms. The rest
Of the time we look at Cécile,
The finest integral work
Of art ever produced north
Of the Alps, a palisade
Of sequoias, the Karnak
Of Europe, the behemoth
Of orthodoxy that devoured
Langue d'Oc. And as the days go by,
The smoke of the Dominicans
Frying the population,
And the curses of the gunman
De Montfort, and the leaking
Pus of Papal hypocrisy
Form a film between the red
Brick cylinders, so noble
And aloof, and my eyes. I
Remember every day that
This fortress church is the symbol
Of the repression of all
That I love in France. The struggle
Of the vine, the olive, and the
Orange against coal, iron, and wool,
The lure of the narrow seas,
The soot of Flanders and the Rhine,
Against the clean blue classic sea.

Unless we can find somewhere
In the course of rebirth the
Realization of all
Persons through the transcendence
Of the self, what I have called
Extrapersonalization,
We must go on mopping the sea,

Quantitatively again
And again reorganizing
The universe of consequence
And possibility in terms
Of our appetites until we
Have entered into personal
Relations with every person
Who now appears as only
One of the electrons of
The present universe.

Rabasson, a filthy church
In a filthy village, the
Fourteenth-century frescoes
Like a healthy Puvis, sweet
As pictures in a child's bedroom,
De Monvel's Jeanne, but honest.

Crossing from the Tarn to the
Garonne, a black storm gathers
In the Pyrenees, breaks up
And lifts over the warm valley
And piles up against the Massif.
Only fringes of its skirts
Brush us as we race down miles
Of hills to Toulouse. Bright lightning
And quick thunder to the east,
And glimmers and murmurs over
The Pyrenees, and great white
Exploding drops in the late sun
So that you think for a moment,
"Here comes the hail." And at last
In twists of wind, hail does come and
Almost hammers us off our
Vélos just as we bump onto
The cobbles of Toulouse.

The true capital of France,
Toulouse like a happier,
Freer Spanish city, like

Mexico, or Los Angeles
Before the Baptists came.
Cassoulet with dark goosemeat
And Tolosian sausage, and
The faint flavor of saffron
And garlic, a formidable
Dessert and the wine of Toulouse,
Dry, bitter goat cheese from the
Pyrenees, and dense sweet coffee
Full of sparks like Italy.
All the leafy city—the
Allées and boulevards and parks
And squares full of bright hurrying
People, an atmosphere as
Bracing as nineteen-twenty in
Chicago. How infinitely
Better off the modern world
Would be if Raimon had won
Instead of the Pope's gangster
And the king of the Isle de France.
Saint Sernin Gaudi's grandfather—
The split personality
Of the cathedral a symbol
Of the conquered city. An
Immense piscine where we
Swim until exhausted and
Bicycle home in the scarlet
Evening, the pale green moon
Over the red brick buildings.
In the museum some fine
Romanesque sculpture, some carved
Capitals, very Byzantine,
With Biblical figures like
The Four Kings at San Marco.
An American male torch-
Singer in the main café.
Black-haired, black-eyed whores with heavy
Gold earrings, full-fleshed in thin
Translucent summer dresses.

France fell at Appomattox.
Louis Napoleon had schemed
For a Mediterranean
Union, a commonwealth of Greece,
Spain, Turkey, Egypt, Italy.
In a generation the
British could have gone back to woad.
To flatter his wife and keep
Austria quiet on the
Adriatic, he bet on
Maximilian and the South.
Grant knew how to fight with railroads,
Juarez's bullets murdered
The last chance of a Latin
Roman Empire, Napoleon
Succumbed to the industrial
And banking North and bit Bismarck,
And that was the end of France.

At last we leave, bicycle
Through villages each with a
Red brick church with bells in a
Pierced gable, what we call "Mission,"
Out past Villefranche and camp
On the Canal du Midi under
The ancient plane trees; full moon;
Great Romanesque farmhouses
Each with an attached arched barn;
A bridge and lock; an old village
Across it; the silver canal
Curving away through black shadows
Of the dense trees; and at dawn
The quiet barges swishing past.

The person is transcended
By the reflection of himself
In the other in love, the
Unique is universalized
In the dual, any important

Crux of reality is
Only the emergence of
A person into a love
Perspective, experience
Has no other real content.

Heavy bicycling all morning,
Down hill in second gear against
A pounding southeast wind from the
Mediterranean, millions
Of cubic miles of transparency
With millions of tons of pressure
Rushing up from Africa.
At the watershed they change the
Trees on the canal to cypress
Because of the constant wind.

In Carcassonne a wistful young
Algerian silver miner
From the Pyrenees who finds
Us a place for lunch at three o'clock,
Incredible in France, and who
Begs us to stay with him that night
And tries to pay for our lunch.
Up to buggery or worse,
No doubt, but very touching.
The castle a tiresome visite.

Quillan, a fête in progress,
No one will feed or house us
In town, a fine restaurant
Under great trees, off on the
Highway, regal food and Blanquette
De Limoux, better than champagne,
Soft sheep cheese and sexual pears
And bunches of the new grapes,
Armagnac like Spanish brandy
And black Levantine coffee.
The Pyrenees and the moon and

The rushing river out the window.
Dancing in the jam-packed streets until
Almost dawn, and then out of town
On the vélos, we camp in
A pinewood, moonblades on the
Loud mountain water, the smell
Of the dry pines parching the nose.

The universe of persons
Is reflected in me as
The inexhaustible content
Of experience, as a
Mountain is reflected in
A mirror or as the moon
In water held in the hand.

Thunderstorms in the Pyrenees.
Very few of the peasants
Speak anything but perfect
Textbook French, all the dialects
Of France are fading away
Before the conquering State.

History assumes the State
As the extrapersonal
Vehicle of memory.
What is important is what is
Held in the sieve of polity.
The State is the great forgetter.

High in the mountains one of the
Few screen doors in France, bright brand new
Copper, and near the sill a neat
Hole cut out for the cat.

Perpignan really like Latin
America, a pleasant, dusty,
Meaningless town. Two fatigued
Merlans for lunch, but saffron
In the rice, and southern wine.

Nightbound, we camp on the Etang
De Solces, mosquitoes in dense clouds
And flies that bite out pieces.
The primus fails, impossible
To reach the sea and swim, we
Fill the tent with DDT spray
And crawl in in spite of the thick heat,
Drink macabeu and go to sleep.
Next morning we encourage
The primus and cook last night's
Risotto for breakfast and drink
The rest of the macabeu.

My knowledge of the others is
Of all grades of indirection.
Love provides an object which may
Be known more and more directly.
In the sex act it may be
Known fully and directly
But only for so brief a time.

Narbonne, the first city of Gaul,
Ruined by the Pope, de Montfort,
And the French king, the cathedral
Only a grandiose choir,
All that was ever finished.
We have Narbonnese honey
At lunch, and find some real ice cream.

Béziers, here de Montfort butchered
Twenty thousand in one day.
The fortress church looms over the
Orb and the Plateau des Poètes.

Cette on its hill in the sea
Marshes, orange and cream-colored
Seventeenth-century houses
Doubled in the glassy canals.
Montpellier busy as
A city in America.

On into Nîmes, the best taste
Of Rome left in the world, fountains
And columns, boulevards and
Terraced water, all the city
Emanating from the old
Temple, as classical as Bath
But not compulsive about it.
Here at last is one place untouched
By the Normans or the English,
No sign of Gothic mentalism—
In fact, the best looking church
Is modern Romanesque. They say
The city was once Calvinist,
Now it seems hardly Christian.
Splendid food, a masterwork
Of a pâté truffé which the
Host carries about like a
Newborn baby, cèpes dipped in
Olive oil and grilled, guinea hen,
Dove, aubergines provençales,
Courgettes stuffed with spiced soft cheese,
Thick crinkly fresh noodles, rice
With saffron, wines like the small wines
Of Naples. The natives put ice in it!

A specialty of Nîmes—
The extraordinarily
Hard-boiled looking whores; like
The girls at Les Halles in Paris
Who circulate amongst the
Flying boxes and vegetables,
Hustling the camion drivers
In the dawn; the same dirty
Bare legs, short skirts, and bobby sox,
Teetering on novelty shoes
In the Jardin de la Fontaine at
Lunch time, their eyes hard in the sun.
Vice during siesta, the touch
Of the Mediterranean.
But where do they come from? Out of
Marseilles for a little rest?

A sudden cold wind at night and
Explosions of lightning and
Rivers of rain, all the lights
In town go out. We stand on
The balcony and watch the trees
And the fountain flash purple white,
And then plunge into black again.
The wind roars, the thunder bangs,
We make love by the open window.

Discursive knowledge, knowledge by
Indirection passes away
And love, knowledge by direction,
Directly of another, grows
In its place. There exists a point
At which the known passes through
A sort of occultation,
A zero between plus and
Minus in which knower and known
And their knowledge cease to exist.
Perfect love casts out knowledge.

The Pont du Gard as beautiful
As ever. Why can't a culture
Of businessmen and engineers
Make beautiful things? I walk
Across on top and then back
Under the small arches with
Idyllic frames of Provence
Slipping past me and suddenly
I notice the shells in the rock—
With my head full of the
Fossils of a million years,
Standing on this fossilized
Roman engineering, built of
Mudflats of fossil seas, springing
From cliffs with caves of fossil man—
Half-naked jeunesse with golden
Bodies scamper over golden
Stone, the air is full of swallows
Whirling above flowing water.

There are three ways of loving,
Modes of communication,
The realization via
The ground of possibility,
We touch each other through the
Material of love, the earth
Center which all share; or by means
Of ultimate inclusive
Action, the empyrean
Shared by all persons where the
Mythology and drama
Of the person is realized
In pure archetype; or face
To face in the act of love,
Which for most men is the way
In which the other modes are
Raised into consciousness and
Into a measure of control.

Provence hot, the hills grey with heat,
Miles of olive trees, silver green,
The color of Sung celadon,
The houses peach colored, over
Each doorway a grape vine, around
It the wall stained pale blue-green with
Copper sulphate spray. Avignon,
Beautiful across the river
But with a god damned visite;
(The legends and chauvinism
Of an ancien combattant,
Permitted, because he has given
A leg or arm to France to beg
In this tedious way. Splendid
Fellows, salty and wise, as who
Wouldn't have to be if this
Was all he got from a grateful
People, but hardly the screen
Through which to absorb The Past.)
And over all the lingering
Stink of the Papacy and
The present stink of English tourists.

The vélos roll down hill, mile
After mile beside rushing
Water into Aix. We go for
A swim in the cold piscine at
The Roman baths and on into
That city of small splendors.

Seldom has man made so perfect
A work of art of light and shade.
The Fromentins are fine in the
Cathedral, but they can't compare
With the green submarine light
Of the Cours Mirabeau broken
By pools of clarity at the
Small fountains at the crossings,
The dark gloom and black statue
Of King René at one end,
The white glare of the Fountain
Of Culture at the other.
Certainly the most civilized
Man ever to get mixed up
With a revolution has
An elegant monument.

The author of *Le Rideau levé*,
Approached as a colleague by
Sade in prison, repulsed him
Succinctly, "Mon Sieur, je ne suis
Pas ici pour avoir donné des
Confits empoisonnés aux femmes
De chambre." The existentialistes
Don't like him very much.

Granet painting in Rome, never
Forgot that light and shade. In
The museum his paintings with
Their stereoscopic values
Hang by his two portraits—
The famous Ingres, more handsome
Than Byron, and another
Of an old, old, dying man.

Lots of Cézanne watercolors
Full of peach blossoms and leaf flicker.

Milhaud, Cendrars, Tal-Coat, a place
Where men with balls can escape
The maggots of the Deux Magots.

Dinner at the Café Mistral,
Plover's eggs and tomatillos
In aspic, écrevisse, raw tuna
With chives, thick noodles with saffron,
Duckling with truffles and cèpes,
Fricassée of guinea hen,
A local wine, not still, not
Sparkling, but volatile like
The chiantis of Florence,
A dark blue cheese, and black, black
Coffee and Rémy Martin
And thick layers of cream—
And then like all the world we
Promenade on Mirabeau's
Fine street and eat glaces and
Drink more cognac and coffee.
At last the strange malady
Of France has vanished and the
Women once more are mammals.

At last the ability to
Know directly becomes a
Habit of the soul and the
Dominant mode in which
Possibility is presented
To the developing person.
As such it ceases to appear
As consequence and becomes
Conscious communion with a
Person. A duality
Is established which focuses
The reflection of the mountain
As an illuminating ray

On the mountain itself,
The moon dissolves in the water
Held in the palm of the hand.

Mile after mile of the fertile
Valleys and the arid mountains
Of Provence. All the world is
Out picking grapes—and great wheeled
Carts in long lines, hauling them
To the wineries. Young peasants
Pelt us with grapes as we ride past.

Fréjus, heavy-breasted and bruised
Whores, Senegalese and Indo-
Chinois soldiers brawl all night
In the streets, even the women
In the shops try to hustle me.

Saint-Raphaël, a California
Town, full of pastry shops and
English children and high-class tarts.
We camp on Cap Rouge and swim
In the warm sea, the Esterels
Over us, the Alps beyond Nice
Coming and going behind
High-piled storm clouds where at night
Sheet lightning wavers like an
Aurora.

        Lunch in Cannes from
Heavy handfuls of bursting fruit.

Agape is built on philia;
Eros on agape; caritas,
The supernatural eros,
On eros; and caritas
Is again the foundation
Of a transformed philia.
Thus the process is a cyclic
Ascent of realms of value.

The vélos stagger in the wind
And we grind into Nice, the
Beverly Hills of the middle
Classes of Europe. A great
Sense of bustling fornication,
Raving beauties in the crowds
Offering themselves for free,
The small type advertisements
In the papers one long epic
Of classified eroticism—
"Tall, striking blonde, properly
Gloved and shod, desires exchange
Lessons in English for advanced
Lessons in French, will pay well."
Thank God, for once a city
Without any monuments!
Two days of promenading
And swimming in the sea and
Then the bus to Genova.

Love, like all the sacraments, is a
Miniature of being itself.
All things have an apparent
Meaning and an opposite
Hidden meaning brought forth by fire.
The phoenix and the tortoise,
The dragon and the unicorn,
Man, eagle, bull, and lion.

III

Zoroaster long ago
Said poetry presents us
With apparent pictures of
Unapparent realities.

The sleep which fell on Adam
Was the deep lassitude

Of divine contemplation.
Eve arose, a projection,
From his dreaming heart. Blake
Made a picture of it once.

Diana Marina, my
Favorite on the Italian
Riviera. Quiet, few
People, no foreigners.
We pass through the town and stop at
An albergo on the river.
The terrace overlooks the sea,
And we swim before dinner
In the sunset Mediterranean.
The owner is a fisherman.
He rows away, standing up,
And looking forward, Italian
Style, into pink and blue space.
We are too happy to be hungry.
We eat only pasta and wine,
Grignolino, the first blood
Of the South. As the padrona
Fills out my card, she says, "San
Francesco, eh? Giannin' è mort'
Oggi," in a sepulchral voice and
Passes me the Genova paper.
I must admit she moves me. It's a
Personal tragedy for her.
I walk in the early evening
On the empty spianato
And turn into town. In a
Very San Francisco-like
Café and billiard room I
Have that best of all heavy
Brandies, Vecchia Romagna.
After France, the toilet seems
As clean as a laboratory.
The streets are wide for Italy,
And the houses square and trim,
Like the seventeenth-century

Ones on the Piazza Navona.
The streets are flagged and all they need
Are the crossing blocks to look
Exactly like Pompeii.
Fireflies are dipping and
Wavering in thin clouds of
Sparkle two feet thick over
All the pavements. In the red
Light district, the beautiful
Deep breasted, long legged, regal
Necked Italian whores are
Wading with elegant carriage
Knee deep in glittering fireflies.

Poetry like the unclouded
Crystal and the uncut block,
And the details of the mirage of life,
Presents contemplation
With its instruments. Then isn't
Contemplation a kind of judgment?
It is all the judgment there is.
The others are paranoia.

As the Philosopher says,
The process of developing
Life complicates but enriches
The world. The process of thought
Simplifies but eviscerates
It. Contemplation is the
Preeminent process of
Developing life; yet it
Follows the form and movement
Of thought. Hence it both unifies
And enriches, and overcomes
The conflicting one and many.
Universalization
Of contemplation is wisdom.
Contemplation is the final
Form of responsibility,
The only truly effective
Mode, and source of all others.

There is no difference between
Love and contemplation as far
As the actual reality
Is concerned. What is taken in
In contemplation is poured out
In love. Love, as a description
Of the process, is the truer
Term because the person
Is more adequately defined.

Genova hot and roaring,
Considerably uglier than
Ashtabula or Gary.
Two coy lions guard the Duomo.
A comprehensive of Magnasco—
"Bad artists dislike painting
Dogs and horses, and prefer
Dragons, demons, and spirits."
A painter for the American
Fairies. A dock strike, Togliatti
Worrying the government,
Ragged workers and double
Breasted bureaucrats, nobody
Seems to know what it is about.
They do what they are told.
Spaghetti, boiled beef, cold
Fagiolini, black grapes, and
Purple inky wine in the
Ristorante Comunale.
We come in late, so all the
Waitresses and their lingering
Boy friends practice up their English.
Everybody very happy
To discover Americans
Who are not rich. My copy
Of *Umanità Nuova*
Creates a tremendous sensation.
Genovese art is dull, the most
Impressive things in town are
The old banking houses, one
Of the finest, with immense

Lanterns and elaborate
Ironwork, now the offices
Of Signor Giannini, the
Cavour of the Second World War,
Nonentity's new arrivéd guest.

The political innocence
Of the Italians is shown
In the fact that every city
Has a Via Cavour. The waste
Of history. Get what you can.
If you don't, somebody
Else will. "Entia non sunt
Multiplicanda praeter
Necessitatem," said Pilate.

The lover and the beloved
Rise above the levels of
Appetite, discursive knowledge,
Consequence, probability,
And enter into each other
Directly. Knowledge of each
Other becomes a mode of
Being, and through each other
The being of all the others
Is realized more and more
Directly. The lover first
Divorces himself from all
Desire to use the beloved.
This means divorcing himself
From all appetite for things.
If the lover desires only
Union with the beloved, and
Desires nothing else, he has
Nothing left to use the beloved
For except herself. The naked
Mutual being is enough
To satisfy all life's desires.
Love is mutual indwelling
Without grasping. It is knowledge
Of another as a state of

Being rather than a process.
Possession and being possessed
Are not a part of love. Indwelling
Is not possession. One does not
Possess oneself. The contract
Relationship of civilized
Love is lust, the balancing
Of possessive appetites.

The will to live or the will to
Power or the will to love.

The fire of the sexual act,
The wedding of light and darkness,
Boehme's scream and flame, the pregnant
Echo of the sound of eternity.

All the highway crowded with
Bicyclists and strolling couples.
Above Shelley's bay the olive
Hills fall away in terraces,
All under the trees, couples as
Beautiful as Praxiteles,
Fucking in the silvery shade,
In the hot perfumed air of
Pentecoste, celebrating
The descent of the dual flame.
We wait, in company with
Miles of cars and busses, high
On the ridge above Rapallo,
Beside a peasant rococo
Church we expect to suddenly
Start revolving and tinkling,
While the Communist Party
Uses the steep highway for a
Motorbike race. Rapallo—
Far worse than treason or dementia,
Pound endured this Atlantic City
Of Czechoslovak yachtsmen and
Swiss gamblers for twenty-five years!

Between the strips of grain are lines
Of poplars with vines growing
On a demountable trellis
Seven feet high. In other parts
Of Italy the vines grow
Directly on the mulberries.
Virgil says elm is the best,
But that was before they raised silk.

Viareggio, maybe the world's
Best beach resort. Nobody
There but Italians, quiet, clean,
Orderly, graceful, no rolly
Coasters, clip joints, or Shriners,
But lots of ice cream, coffee,
Brandy, good food, white sand, and
The warm and gentle purple sea.
During the war a regiment
Of boys from old Southern families
Was quartered in town.
Giosi says, as we walk in the
Moonlit pinewood, "Man, yo right down
In front. Man, ah relly dig yo.
Ah means, yo groovy, yo send me!"
She talks this way all the time
Under the impression she is
Speaking the English language.

It is the essence of love
To transcend consequence. Love
Is the total act of the
Person, all other activity
Is contributory to
The act of love, which is the
Special and definitive
Act of the person. That is
What a person is, a lover.

Having never read any of
These "Lost Art Treasures" books,

At Pisa we run across the lawns
To the Campo Santo, open
The door and rush inside. The shock
Is too much for me and I drop
Onto a bench made of a
Roman capital and gasp with pain.
An old gentleman, looking much
Like Victor Emmanuel, comes
Over and pats me on the head.
"Si, si, si, war is horrible.
You did not know the frescoes were
Gone? The Inglesi. Everywhere
In Italia they have
Destroyed the monumenti.
The Tedeschi and the Americani
Were careful, but the Inglesi
Are jealous of Italia.
Even today they are still
At war with us."

Cardinals
Saying vespers in the Duomo.
Isaiah's wizards who peeped
And muttered behind the altar.
But, says the judgment, "My hands shall
Find as a nest the riches
Of the people; and as one
Gathereth eggs that are left,
Shall I gather all the earth;
And none shall move the wing or
Open the mouth, or peep."

Here Pound
Stumbled to the pitiful
Conclusion of the longest
And most highly decorated
Hymn of hate in literature.

How easy it is to hate
A people who claim all the

Mundane advantages of a
Supernatural community
And carefully deny all the
Transcendental responsibilities.
Everybody tries it, as
Max Weber points out, but no one
So successfully as the Jews,
Who hurt only themselves.

"I can get it for you wholesale."
In fact, the Jewish middle class
Do it better than the Masons
Or the Knights of Columbus, quite
Automatically. The poor,
Far from B'nai Brith, deep down
Underground from the Talmud,
Keep the ancient communion,
The pagan sensual bond,
Older than the Torah, old as
The new moon on the sacred pillar.
The atomized, secularized
Gentile wage slave can be excused
A little wistful envy.

Ancient Hebrew religion
Was essentially orgiastic,
In the sense that mystical
Fulfillment, the actual
Worship of the gods, consisted
In the physical act of
Begetting children before the
Lord. At the climax of sexual
Union, the goddess Shekinah,
Jehovah's embodied Glory,
Was made manifest over the
Marriage bed, coupled with her
Divine lover. It was from
Their union, really, that the seed
Of Israel descended to
The womb of the enraptured wife.

Post-exilic Judaism
Extracted from this mystic
Orgiastic cult only its
Ritual prohibitions
And injunctions, robbed of content.
The ancient religion survived
Occulted in the Kabbalah
And Chasidism, and in the
Stubbornly held folkways of
The Ghetto. For instance, the
Roofs of the little arbors
Built in the backyard to this day
By good Jews on the Feast of
The Great Mother, are purposely
Only a scant openwork,
So that she may descend and
Possess the husband and wife as they
Make love under the new moon.

In the shadow of the lingam
And yoni, the massebah,
On the feast of oil and wine,
From the arbors of Asiph,
From the embracing lovers,
Joy spread like a sweet incense
In the fire of communion.
Then the virgins of Israel,
Adorned with tabrets, went forth
In the dances of them that
Make merry. Then the winepress
Was trod with joy and gladness.
There was shouting at the vintage.
When the daughters of Shiloh
Came out to dance in dances,
The men came from the vineyards,
And every man took a bride.

She answered me so gaily,
She seemed to burn in love's first flame,
"Brother, our will is stilled by

The power of love which makes us
Wish only for what we have
And thirst for nothing else."

"Long as the feast of Paradise,
So long our love shall wrap us
In the rays of such a garment.

Brightness shall follow our ardor,
Ardor, our vision. All shall be
Gracious with its true value.

Here we do not repent, but smile
Not at sin which never comes to mind,
But at the value which orders

And provides. The love which moves
All being, penetrates the
Universe, and shines back, in

Some things more, in others, less."

When the Romans hunted him
Who had dared to speak against them,
Simon ben Johai took his son,
Eleazar, and they hid
Buried to their necks in a
Cave for fourteen years and a
Miracle fed them. And when
They came out the son's eyes burned
The mundane works of men with
Transcendental wrath, but the word
Of the father restored them.
And an ancient peasant came
And presented them with two sprays
Of myrtle. And Eleazar
Smelled them and found them perfumed
With the odors of Paradise.
And Simon ben Johai said,
"It is the perfume of the

164

Hidden bride in heaven, the
Sabbath, the cloud of glory."
And Eleazar remembered
The bride wreaths of Israel.
And his father said to him,
"This is the work which the Lord
Has made, let us rejoice and
Be glad in it." And they went
To Rome and healed the daughter
Of the Emperor of the
Devil which had entered her.

Antisemitism is
An exceptional folly
In the roster of lunacy.
Actually, the power
Of the rabbinate has been
So absolute that the Jew
Has wasted millennia
Tangled in a meaningless
Legalism and has not
Functioned as a social
Or economic competitor
Of the Gentile world at all.
The Elders of Zion doubtless
Conspired, but only to enslave
And make impotent their own race.
Once I had the sentimental
Hope that some of the old ways
Would come back in Palestine
In the secular kibutzim.
But today ex-radical
And liberal Jews call Buber
A crypto-Christian and traitor
To his blood, and go to parties
At the homes of rich and silly
Women, and hop around by
Candle light, making noises
Like Fanny Brice, while a
Grimjawed, double-breasted

Bureaucrat gathers in the take.
What price Utopia in dollars?
A kibutz for every taste.
Down the chute to destruction, the
Last bourgeois nationalism.

Who is the "English King" buried
At Lucca? An historical
Mystery like the Chartres
Fellow, come home to die after
A life spent in High Asia
In the service of the Great Khan.

After Chase and Sanborn's coffee
At Leland's Bar, the American
Fairies cruise the Lungarno,
Hunting tall, broadshouldered, hungry
Florentines. At the local court
Of the king and queen of the set
Who commute between Florence
And Tangiers, a party for
Their world's leading poet.
My mother used to say, "A snob
Is a person who mimics the
Manners of those above him."
All the hell of American
Italy. I look in the door
And flee back to Florence, and run
Into miles of Communists
Marching under the immense icons
Of Stalin, Molotov, Togliatti,
And
     MAO TSE TUNG
     POETA E GUERRIERO

I am convinced the Dogana
Allows no heterosexual
American under forty
Past the Italian border.

Under the arcades of the Uffizi
At night lie sleeping family
After family, cuddled
Around their babies. In the
Piazza, the orchestra
Plays *La Vie en rose.* The waiter
Gives me my change—the first new coins
Stamped "Republica Italiana."
Boethius and Theodoric,
Dante and Machiavelli,
Rienzi, Emperors, and Popes,
Arnold of Brescia, Federigo,
Are as dead as Mazzini.
The long pain of history
In my heart is too much for me.
The blonde wife of the band leader
Sings, "Mene, mene, tekel, upharsin."

Why this sudden outburst of
Homosexuality?
The American mass culture
Has identified the normal
Sex relation with the stuffing
Of an omnivorous and
Insensate vagina with
Highly perishable and
Expensive objects of non
Utility. Useless value
Has replaced use value and has
Been linked with sex satisfaction.
Since every young American
Male knows that very soon the State
Is going to take him out and
Murder him very nastily,
He is inclined to withdraw from
The activities prescribed for him
In the advertising pages.
Since it is physically
Impossible to realize

The fullness of love except
Between a man and woman,
This is at best a sort of
Marking time before execution.
For similar reasons, children
In the highschools take heroin.
Why not? They gave Christ narcotics
On the cross. You cannot expect
To terrify children with
Atom bomb drills and quiet them
With Coca-Cola. During the
Last months of the Second War,
The Japanese had begun
An experimental, routine
Administration of shock
Therapy to all combat troops.
Only the decorticated
Will be able to survive the
Last horrors of the profit system.
French radical youth, like
The Wandervögel before them,
Have a better way of marking
Time until the monsters destroy
Each other: Keep uncompromised;
Stay poor; try to keep out from
Under the boot; love one another;
Reject all illusions; wait.
"Antisemitism" said
Marx, "Is the socialism of
Fools." Homosexuality
Is the revolt of the timid.

Boswell: "Sir, what is the chief
Virtue?" Johnson: "Courage, Sir,
Without it, opportunity
To exercise the others
Will often be found wanting."

On his first visit to the States,
Wells was asked what most impressed him.

He said, "The female schoolteachers.
In two generations they will
Destroy the country." It took one.

In the Uffizi I prefer
To spend most of my time with the
Even tempered Greeks and Romans.
Pictures in galleries always
Look to me like dressed meat in
Butcher shops. From Cimabue
And Simone Martini,
Arrows point across the river
To Bronzino, and via
Raphael, to Picasso.
Without Florence, there isn't
Really any modern painting,
But just the same, it looks cooked.
Straight through, from beginning to end,
It is all Mannerism.
In the churches you get tired
Of all the Taddis and Gaddis.
Why does no one ever point out
That the great Masaccios are
Compounded of the elements
Of Roman painting, and no
Others at all, and that each figure
Is derived from classic sculpture?
There is the same knowledge of
Good and evil, and in the face
Of it, the same serenity.

God is that person who
Satisfies all love, with whom
Indwelling encompasses
All reality. It is
Impossible to say if there
Exists only one god, the
Ultimate beloved of all
Persons. It would seem rather,
Since the relationship is

169

Reciprocal and progressive,
That there are as many gods
As lovers. Theoretically
One infinite god could
Satisfy all finite lovers—
But this concept comes from the
Insoluble residues of
The quantitative mathematics
Of infinitudes. It really
Has no place in the discussion
Of the love relationship,
Which knows neither finite nor
Infinite. The Shekinah
And Jehovah are only
An enlarged mirror image
Of the terrestrial embrace.
The sephiroth of the Kabbalah
Are the chakras of the Tantra.
The records of Hafidh, Rumi,
St. Theresa, even the crazed
Augustine, seem to be the
Records in each case of a
Unique duality. The
Object of love is a person
Like the lover, and the demands
On the definition of
A monotheistic god
Made by other philosophical
Considerations, largely
Of an arithmetical
Nature, make it unlikely
That such an entity could be
Also a person. There is here a
Collision of two exclusive
Modes of viewing reality.
Hence perhaps the peculiar
Subjective tension of the
Monotheistic mystic,
The reason why he always feels
His love as incomplete and
Destructive of his person.

Agathias Scholasticus:
Restless and discontent
I lie awake all night long.
And as I drowse in the dawn,
The swallows stir in the eaves,
And wake me weeping again.
I press my eyes close tight, but
Your face rises before me.
O birds, be quiet with
Your tittering accusations.
I did not cut that dead girl's tongue.
Go weep for her lover in the hills,
Cry by the hoopoe's nest in the rocks.
Let me sleep for a while, and dream
I lie once more in my girl's arms.

Under a lattice of leaves
Her white thighs in cloth of gold
That casts a glittering shade.
She turned to her left and stared at
The sun. My imagination
Was moved by her gesture, and as
I turned, I saw the sun
Sparkle all round, like iron
Pulled molten from the furnace.

Bright petals of evening
Shatter, fall, drift over Florence,
And flush your cheeks a redder
Rose and gleam like fiery flakes
In your eyes. All over Florence
The swallows whirl between the
Tall roofs, under the bridge arches,
Spiral in the zenith like larks,
Sweep low in crying clouds above
The brown river and the white
River bed. Your moist, quivering
Lips are like the wet scarlet wings
Of a reborn butterfly who
Trembles on the rose petal as
Life floods his strange body.

Turn to me. Part your lips. My dear,
Some day we will be dead.

I feel like Pascal often felt.

About the mid houre of the nicht

FIRE

The air is dizzy with swallows.

Sunset comes on the golden
Towers, on the Signoría.
In the Badía, the light goes
From the face of Filippino's
Weary lady, exhausted with
The devotion of her worshipper.
Across the face of the Duomo
The Campanile's blue shadow
Marks the mathematics of beauty.
In San Miniato the gold
Mosaics still glitter through
The smoky gloom. At the end
Of the Way of the Cross, the dense
Cypress wood, full of lovers,
Shivering with impatience.
As the dark thickens, two by two
They take each other. Nightfall, all
The wood is filled with soft moaning,
As though it were filled with doves.

In this way, lifted to this height,
These creatures trace the spoor of
The Eternal Value to the
End and pattern of all things.

The insoluble problems—
The order of nature, the
Ego and the other, the

Freedom of the will, evil,
Identity, time, mind and
Body, indeterminateness,
The economy of nature,
The unity of knowledge,
The principle of conservation,
Essence and existence, form
And content, act and power,
Rest and motion, the one and
The many, all these have no
Meaning in the fulfillment
Of love. All that is, needs, in
Its ultimate reality,
Some sort of definition;
But what we know of its
Apparent character would be
Better described as a
Community of lovers,
Rather than an Absolute
And its aspects, or a Creator
And his contingent creatures.

Maybe the Or' San Michele
Is an architectural
What is it, but every night
We walk around it a couple
Of times before we go home.
I can never forget those
Supple bodies and lithe faces—
In the summer twilight when
"The swallows and the bats change guard,"
In the perfumed smoke of Autumn,
And glazed with chilling rain.
I know of no intact building
Which gives you more of a sense
Of being a part of a
Civilized community.
And there around you on the streets
Are the same beautiful people
With the same potential in them.

As the Philosopher says,
He who contemplates a statue
Shares the thought of the artist;
The statue itself does not.
As the soul contemplates nature,
The spirit the light, and the mind
The stars, every eye sees into
The matrix from which it was born.

We walk by the Arno singing
Cowboy and hillbilly songs.
One night on the Via dei
Servii, I am singing *The
Wreck of the Ninety Seven*
At the top of my voice. When I
Get to the line, "His whistle broke
Into a scream," I go, "WHOO! WHOO!"
And scare a poor civilized
Florentine dog. He jumps straight up,
Rigid with terror, and then goes
Into paroxysms of shrill
Barking that may be lasting yet.

Lawrence, Lawrence, what a lot
Of hogwash you have fathered.
Etruscan art is just plain bad.
It is the commercial art
Of mercenary provincials,
On a par with Australian
Magazine covers. Where it is
Good at all, it was done by Greeks.
True, something of the secret
Prehomeric world lingers, but
Probably a little bit of
Homer lingers in Canberra.
The Hellenistic Chimera
Which all the highbrows disdain
Is a better organized horror,
And the Apollo of Veii
A better hierophant of the

Great Mother of Crete and the Isles,
Than anything the natives did.
And by far the best Etruscan
Architect was Thomas Jefferson.

An enormous amount of
Misplaced ingenuity,
Especially since the rise of
Capitalist Protestantism,
With its "existential anguish,"
Has gone to the reducing
Of each basic context or
Description of experience
To a dilemma, and then
Resolving the dilemma
By calling it resolved, and
Calling the resolution
God. Actually our descriptions
Of experience run out
Into a very patent
Dilemma—experience itself,
Which is not exhaustible
By quantitative description,
And which is its own context.
Experience, to be known, must,
Obviously, be experienced.
The purely logical culs-
De-sac adduced as proofs of God
Are unworthy of the subject.
God is lover and beloved—a
Person—or he is nothing
Important. I see no way
Of proving his nonexistence,
But there is no way of proving
That the person experienced
By all the lovers of God
Is actually the same person,
And if the only absolute
Is a community of equals,
There is no room for him.

Experience is the
Manifestation of persons
One to another. It is
Possible for all experience
To be absorbed and evalued
By the manifestation of
One person, and all other
Persons and their manifestations
Seen only through the one lover.
But this is precisely the end
Of all persons—the opening
Of the Summum Bonum, the
Beatific Vision, and is
Found in the plenum of love,
The interlocking manifold
Of dualities, not in a monist
Absolute and its contingent beings.

San Lorenzo in Perugia—
A jewel box restored with
An exquisite sense of chic,
Which could not quite overcome
The strange, sterile, diseased murals
Of Aliense, that well-named painter—
Full of chairs for a concert,
The front rows marked "CINEASTI."
A little door behind the
Altar. Fiat Lux! Assisi
Far away on its hill in the
Blazing air of Umbrian Summer.
At the Ristorante Comunale,
A fine Umbrian ham, mast fed,
Flesh like the game of Artemis.
When I tell an American
Where I eat, he acts as though
I had just come from Smolny Institute,
And never speaks to me again.

This brings up the question, are
The other human beings,

176

The people around us who
Seem part of the unreal things
Of time and space, only more
Active, real? Are they all persons,
Potential objects of our love?
This question has no real meaning.
It is like, "Is compassion green?"
When viewed as part of the world
Of quantity, no. Just as the
Bursting of bombs, the falling
Of leaves or stars, are the voices
Of some person speaking to us,
Are perspectives on a person,
So the figures of clothed bipeds
Which surround us are similar
Perspectives. We assume from
Experience that if approached,
The person will in each case
Be present, usually more
Accessible than in the leaf
Or star. However, as part
Of the world of consequence
And possibility, "this crowd
Of men" is illusory.

Arezzo, a fine commercial
Hotel, our bedroom ceiling
Covered with Turks and tigers.
Splendid gnocchi and heady wine—
Montepulciano—strong for lunch.
After a day immersed in the
Lucid systems of Piero,
I realize that he had
The first true neoclassic mind,
Anti-expressive and hence
Expressive of every strange
Cold torture of the regular
Beating of the orderly heart.
Constantine's "we worship

177

Cold water and the moon, beaten
By the hawk's wings of vision."
Baudelaire might have painted it.

Siena, two American
Fairies sipping brandy before
The Cathedral, all the urchins
Crying, "Milioni! Milioni!"
Heady stuff for boys from Texas,
Especially just after lunch.
Sienese painting was so suave,
So civilisé, so sick,
So early doomed. The Southern
Sung were like this, but they managed
To keep it a good deal cleaner.
Rossetti knew his parents.

For the undeveloped heart,
The news or even the sight
Of the destruction of thousands
Of other human beings
May assume only the form
Of a distant cry, coming
Through the complexities of
Disaster, of one other
Person. An air raid may be
Only a distraction from
A letter to a sweetheart;
The famines and floods of China
Only transportation
Difficulties between hotels.
However, as the dual,
The beloved, is known and
Loved more and more fully, all
The universe of persons
Grows steadily more and more real.
Eventually loss or pain
To the least of these, the most
Remote known person of the
Other, is felt personally

Through the intense reality
Of the dual. There is no
Way of proving the existence
Of a person except by
Experience, but we assume
The appearance "human being"
Is always, at least potentially,
The immediate vesture
Of a person. None the less,
It must not be forgotten
That, as such, this appearance is
Only a sign of possible
Underlying reality
In a manifold of empty
Contingency. There is no
Self subsistence whatever
In the manifold as such.

A girl nun, praying cruciform,
Her face pressed against the
Portiuncula, suddenly
Utters a high, hawk-like scream
And faints. Over this blackened
Dolmen of love rises a
Monstrous vulgar church, worse than
Anything to be found in
America or Australia.

Assisi like a warm Lhasa.
To see the Giottos you buy light
By the minute from a slovenly
Franciscan. How little atheist
Sentimentalists know of this
Rotten, corrupt, dirty, venal,
Mercenary, and ignorant
Order, which has spent
Eight hundred years murdering
Its founder with at least
As conspicuous success as
The Christians have managed with Christ.

Intellectuals who admire
The architectonics of
Neo-Thomism, the liturgics
Of Solesmes, forget that they
Are not the expression of
A living church, but carefully
Constructed booby traps of
Archaism built by over-
Sophisticated Anglican
And Gallican agnostics.
From Newman and Duchesne
To Maurras and Daudet, the entire
Structure of fashionable
Neo-Catholicism has
Been declared heretical at
Each step of its evolution.
This is not Rome. The true face of
Rome is to be seen in Naples,
Franco's Spain, Santo Domingo.

In softheaded America,
Pseudo liberal folly
Has now reached such a pitch, it
Is considered unprogressive
To criticize the Papacy.

Trasimeno in thick mist.
Hannibal and the Romans
Struggle invisibly all
Around us. Midway of the lake
The mist vanishes, and we
Look back into the turquoise
Morning. Villages, castles,
Fields, not a soul moving in
All the brilliance. It might be
Painted on gold leaf and gesso.

Soracte. I guess things were
Different in those days.
Now it is all arid squalor.

I would as soon have a farm
In the Salinas Valley.
Two vast hieratic oxen
Drowsily guard the approach
To a dismal shack, "BAR HORATIO."
As we come down the highway
Through suburbs much like Cleveland,
The Tiber appears, and then a sign,
"PONTE MILVIO." We enter
Rome in the tracks of the first
Triumph of barbarism
And religion, through crowding
Ghosts from Piero's fresco.

It was Rome on the fifteenth
Of October, as I sat
Musing amidst the ruins
Of the Capitol, while the
Barefoot friars were singing vespers
In the Temple of Jupiter—

Gibbon in Rome, Polybius
In Carthage, and Strabo in
Babylon, myself in New York.
The pomp and grandeur of evil
Soon passes, but always a new
Pustule opens somewhere on the earth.
Why should time come to an end?
The stars eat their own feces.
Hunger gives rise to series and
Series gives rise to consequence.

We live in the Pensione
San Giorgio, on the Piazza
Sant' Apostoli, an island
Of quiet in a city
As noisy as Newark, in the
Palace of Cardinal York,
The last legitimate Stuart
Claimant to the English throne.

The whole Piazza was once
A sort of little England.
Here Alfieri cuckolded
Bonnie Prince Charlie. Here the Old
Pretender set his jaw and died.
Here is the best beer in Rome,
And two of the best restaurants.
Although it is just around the
Corner, you can escape from the
World's largest wedding cake, which
Follows you all over town.

It didn't take the Renaissance
Long to find out that the Christian
Documents can be read in a
Kabbalistic sense, but the
Gospels, and especially Paul,
Can also be read as a new
Colonial policy for
Rabbinical Judaism.
An orgiastic religion
Is not easily centralized,
And almost impossible to
Bureaucratize. The declining
Roman Empire left thousands
Of bureaucrats unemployed.
Naturally they chose orthodox
Catholicism which was
Willing to compromise and
Absorb any ritual or doctrine
As long as it could be given
A new content—the power
Of the underemployed
Intellectuals of Rome.
Caiaphas assumed the triple
Crown—or the bloodthirsty Stoic
Philospher Seneca—
It makes no difference—
A few generations later,
He would have been Pope.

San Clemente, a layer cake
Of the decay of mystery—
On top a Catholic church,
Below it, a Christian church,
Under the earth, a Mithraeum.

From the Middle Ages on,
With few exceptions the art of
Rome is WPA art.
It isn't as bad as the
Buckwheat cake Sumerian
Bas reliefs of the history
Of education and science,
With which Roosevelt flooded These States,
But only because he had poorer
Material to begin with.
But it is obvious that
Every artist or architect
Who went to work for the Pope
Knew in advance he had sold out.
Only Raphael remained
Uncorrupted, but Raphael,
Like his archangelic namesake,
Was too pure to be a moral
Agent. Even the painting
Of the Counter Reformation—
The Pope's very own expression—
Is compromised. The Jesuit
Ceilings are not Tiepolo,
They are Tiepolo's mummy.
There are a few islands, the
Piazza Navona, where
Bernini for once stopped acting
Like a giddy matron, perhaps
The Lateran, which compares
Very favorably with the
Railroad station in Washington.
Of course there are the early
Mosaics, and the unchanged
Spaces of the basilicas,

And one little hidden church.
And there are always the great Greeks
And Romans. They must have been
Really a little like Plutarch
Describes them. We sit on the
Floor all afternoon in front of
The Ludovisi throne, and there's
The little flapper with her
New hair-do, and those haunted
Paintings in the Vatican,
Where Tanguy got, and spoiled, his stuff.
The critics tell you the Romans
Couldn't paint, and all that survives
Is provincial commercial art.
This may be very true, but
No other prosperous farmer
Known to history decorated
His walls like the Villa dei
Misterii. It doesn't
Matter, Fra Angelico
To Pontormo, some disorder
Of the conscience, some lesion
Of the sensibility,
Drove them to act up, to try
To exorcise with magic
The dilemmas of life in
This hard universe. Life cannot
Be outwitted. The Romans
Never act up. They miss no
Lie, no horror, and their judgments
Are as worldly and as
Devastating as the Roman Law.

In the Hebrew religion
There could be no mystical
Experience without marriage—
Kedeshim and Kedeshoth,
Every man and wife together.
Therefore each family became
A separate unit in the

Community of Israel.
The hierarchy of the Church
Forbade illumination
To all but celibates, and
Centralized authority
Under celibate bishops.
Sexual fulfillment became
Treason to the bureaucracy.
Heresy—all normal life
Seeking its normal end—went
Underground. When it reappeared
In the political vacuum
Of Provence for a brief moment,
The bureaucracy liquidated
Its practitioners, "as a class,"
In history's bloodiest purge
Before the invention of progress.
However, in France, the Church
Was forced to tolerate a new
Morality. Whenever it could
It debased it to common
Promiscuity. Cardinals
And Kings were little better than
Whoremasters, but the Freemasons
Who led the French Revolution
Were both erotic mystics and
Political libertarians.
Rochester may have been perverse
When he translated the hymns
Of a jealous god into
Songs to his mistress. Mirabeau
Meant business with his Sophie.

Michelangelo was surely
A noisy man, and terribly
Conceited. After all, nothing
Ever happened to him that
Doesn't happen to all of us.
If you have tragedy to
Portray, you should be humble

About it, you are serving
The bread of communion.
"Too many nakeds for a chapel,"
Said Evelyn. But I don't think it
Was the exposed privates of the
Mother of God made the Pope faint.
That's an arrogant, perverse, pride
Soaked wall, a good thing to look down
On the election of the Popes.
Maybe he intended it for
A portrait of the Papacy.
But the Moses was beautiful
Just before the church shut, looking
Like oiled ivory against
The wavering blackness in
The light of the vigil lamps.

The worship of art, the attempt
To substitute it for religion,
Is the blindest superstition
Of them all. Almost all works of
Art are failures. The successes
Occur hardly once in a
Lifetime even in periods
Of great cultural flowering;
And then they are likely to be
Unpretentious perfections,
Of modest scope, exquisite
As a delicate wine and
Often no more significant.
Better lump them all together—
"A good judge of wine, women,
And horseflesh"—than go posting
For the Absolute in the
Galleries of Fifty-seventh Street—
Or the Louvre—or the Uffizi.
The World's Masterpieces are
Too often by Vasari,
Benjamin West, Picasso,
Or Diego Rivera.

The Pope was once content to rule
The rulers, the masses were
Allowed their old worship under
A new nomenclature. Feudal
Methods of exploitation
Required a homogeneous
Society, a "natural"
Religion. New methods,
New cadres. Capitalism
Revived all the paranoid
Compulsions of rabbinical
Judaism, coupled with
A schizophrenic doctrine
Of the person as utterly
Alone, subsistent as a pure
Integer at the will of a
Uniquely self subsistent
Commander (hardly a lover),
Two things with wills. It required
The total atomization
Of society. The family
Hierarchy disappeared and the
Monogamous couple was
Substituted. Not a vehicle
Of mystic love, but an iron
Necessity for survival.

Says Evelyn, "Turning to the right
Out of the Porta del Popolo,
We came to Justinian's
Gardens, near the Muro Torto,
So prominently built as to
Threaten to fall any moment,
Yet standing so these thousand years.
Under this is the burying
Place of the common prostitutes,
Where they are put into the ground
Sans ceremony." In the
Rotonda Sant' Agostino,
A sign, "Whores will refrain

From hustling the customers
During their devotions." From the
Albergo Inghilterra
To the Piazza di Spagna
Stretches a solid tide wall
Of crew-cut American fairies,
Elderly nymphomaniacs,
Double breasted, gabardined
Artisti. The latter have reduced
Hemingway to a formula.
"Let's go," Bill said. "Let's go," Pete said.
"OK, let's go," Joe said. It's like
Dante's terza rima, and the
Triad of the dialectic.
Honest. They write books about it.
Everybody on the prowl
For Cineasti and Milioni
Of any sex. The Via
Vittorio Veneto
After dark is strictly graded.
On the terrace of the Doni
Sit the condottieri of
The Marshall Plan like Rameses.
The Cineasti and Milioni
Lounge over their highballs.
The artisti stand and bow.
The more expensive whores walk
The sidewalks. The poorer whores work
The side streets. The most expensive
Sit. At the entrance to the
Park are whores from Masereel
And Félicien Rops. Inside are
Italian boys who get paid.
Further inside are beringed
Cigar smoking Italians, who
All look like Mussolini's
Grandfather. They will pay you.
At the beginning of the street
Is the American Embassy.

Midway is an ESSO pump.
At the end is the devouring dark.

"La mauvaise conscience des
Bourgeois, ai-je dit, a paralysé
Tout le mouvement intellectuel
Et moral de la bourgeoisie.
Je me corrige, et je remplace
Ce mot 'paralysé' par
Cet autre: 'dénaturé.' "
So Bakunin says, and Marx,
"The bourgeoisie, wherever
It has got the upper hand,
Has put an end to all feudal,
Patriarchal, idyllic
Relations. It has pitilessly
Torn asunder the motley
Feudal ties that bound man to
His 'natural superiors,'
And has left no other nexus
Between man and man than naked
Self interest, than callous
Cash payment. It has drowned the
Most heavenly ecstasies
Of religious fervor, of
Chivalrous enthusiasm,
Of philistine sentimentalism,
In the icy water of
Egotistical calculation.
It has resolved personal worth
Into exchange value, and in
Place of the numberless
Indefeasible chartered freedoms,
Has set up that single
Unconscionable freedom,
Free trade. In a word, for
Exploitation veiled by
Religious and political
Illusions, it has substituted

Naked, shameless, direct, brutal
Exploitation."
For Dante,
Usury was the ultimate
Form of pederasty, in which
Buggery attempts to make
Its turds its heirs.

Sexual fulfillment was robbed
Of all meaning. The sex act became
A nervous stimulant and
Anodyne outside of the
Productive process, but still
Necessary to it as an
Insatiable, irrational
Drive, without which the struggle
For meaningless abstractions,
Commodities, would collapse.
This is the ultimate in
Human self alienation.
This is what the revolution
Is about. In a society
Ruled only by the cash nexus
The sexual relationship
Must be a continual struggle
Of each to obtain security
From the other, a kind of
Security, a mass of
Commodities, which has no
Meaning for love, and today in
America, no meaning at all.
The greater the mass of things,
The greater the insecurity.
The security of love lies
In the state of indwelling rest.
It is its own security.
This is what free love is, freedom
From the destructive power
Of a society coerced
Into the pursuit of insane

Objectives. Until men learn
To administer things, and are
No longer themselves organized
And exploited as things, there can
Be no love except by intense
Effort directed against
The whole pressure of the world.
In other words, love becomes,
As it was with the Gnostics,
The practice of a kind of cult.
Against it are arrayed all
The consequences of a
Vast systematic delusion,
Without intelligence or
Mercy or even real being,
But with the power to kill.

Centuries ago they tore down
Or remodelled all the best
Churches in Rome. But there is one
Which haunts the mind permanently,
Quattro Santi Coronati,
The only church in Rome where
Otto's sense of the holy
Lingers; a secret place where
Christianity still seems
A mystery religion.
It is perched on a rampart
Between the Esquiline and the
Palatine, and approached by two
Courtyards like a Norman castle.
The ancient frescoes in the
Sacristy chapel are a
Child's innocent idea of
The conversion of a king.
The church is restored and full of
Junk, but the awe is still there.
The Holy Place at Alamut,
The fortress churches of the
Crusaders, Krak, empty and

Sand blown in the empty desert,
Must have been something like this.
The Four Crowned Saints were artists who
Would not make idols for Caesar.

What is Capri to me, or me
To Capri? To Hell with the
Bourgeois scenery, said Gurly
To Big Bill Hayward. We live
Back of the Porta Capuana
Where the adolescent whores
Are too poor to buy stockings,
And rent their sleazy dresses
To each other around the clock,
And turn their tricks on the ground
Like the rug girls in New Orleans.
Twenty per cent of the male
Children of Naples are without
Domicile. An equal number
Have active tuberculosis.
Little girls have virtue, and so
The Church finds them domicile.
In the midst of boiling squalor,
The crazed faces of American
Cover girls on the magazines,
The special devils of this
Proliferating Hell, where
Only the innocent are damned.
In Sorrento the lace makers
Are called apprentices and work
For a bowl of polenta at lunch.
Babies are doped with bromides,
And rented around the clock, like
The whores' dresses, to beggar women.
You never see a beggar's baby
Awake, in a few months it is dead.
But the Church keeps the people
Fruitful, birth control is a
Prison offense. Everybody,
Except the tourists, gives to the

Beggars, the Church teaches Charity.
But they keep only a few
Lire a day, periodically
Boys on bicycles shake them down,
And collect the take for the
Lords of the lazzaroni,
Who pay off to the archbishop.
We go to call on the leading
Anarchist theoretician.
He patriotically denies
That conditions like this exist.
He sits in his expensively
Appointed office and questions
Us about how the theories
Of Wilhelm Reich, and the orgones,
Are doing in America.
I have been further round the shit
Pot looking for the handle
Than this bastard has been from home.
The Hell with him, the Museum
Is full of workers in rags,
Ebullient before the Greek
Statues. Three excited, stinking
Fishermen are having a
Violent argument in front
Of Barberi's portrait of
Luca Pacioli, with its face
Like a pure crystal and its
Crystal like a pure mind. I
Could be happy here. There is
All the world still left to win.

America is today a
Nation profoundly deranged,
Demented, and sick, because
Americans with very few
Exceptions believe, or when
They doubt are terrified to
Be discovered doubting, that
Love is measured entirely

In an interchange of
Commodities. The wife provides
Pop-up toast, synthetic coffee,
Frozen orange juice, two eggs of
Standard color, size, and flavor,
In the morning, at night the
Fantastic highly-colored canned
Poisons which grace the cooking
And advertising pages
Of the women's magazines.
In exchange the husband provides
Her with the clothes and cosmetics
Of a movie courtesan,
A vast array of "labor"
Saving devices, all streamlined,
Presumably so they can be
Thrown, a car, never more than
Two years old, engineered with
Great skill to their social status,
A television set, a dream
House, designed by a fairy,
And built of glass and cardboard,
A bathroom full of cramped, pastel
Tinted plumbing. When they wish
To satisfy their passions,
They go to a movie. The
Sexual relation is
A momentary lapse from
The routine fulfillment of
This vision, which is portrayed
As love and marriage by thousands
Of decorticated and
Debauched intellectuals,
Who enjoy the incomes of princes.
Almost all advertising
In America today
Is aimed at the young married
Couple. Billions are consciously
And deliberately spent

To destroy love at its source.
Like the "fiends" who are picked up
In parks, an advertising
Man is a professional
Murderer of young lovers—
On an infinitely vaster scale.

You will find more peace and more
Communion, more love, in an hour
In the arms of a pickup in
Singapore or Reykjavik,
Than you will find in a lifetime
Married to a middle class
White American woman.

It feels like it's made of plastic.
It smells like it's perfumed with
Coal tar. It tastes like it's made
Of soybeans. It looks like an
Abandoned pee-wee golf course.
It is still and sterile
As a crater on the moon.

Sitting there, reading this in your
Psychoanalyst's waiting room,
Thirty-five years old, faintly
Perfumed, expensively dressed,
Sheer nylons strapped to freezing thighs,
Brain removed at Bennington
Or Sarah Lawrence, dutiful
Reader of the *Partisan*
Review's Book of the Month, target
Of my highbrow publisher, you
Think this is all just Art—contrast—
Naples—New York. It is not. Every time
You open your frigidaire
A dead Neapolitan baby
Drops out. Your world is not crazy.
But dead. It can only mimic

Life with the economics of
Murder. "War production and
Colonialization of
The former imperialist
Centers." This is the definition
Of Fascism. You are not just
Responsible. You are the dead
Neapolitan baby,
The other side of the coin.
I don't wonder you've never
Been the same since you left the
Tickets to *Don Giovanni*
In the orgone collector.

At the Pappagallo, cold squid,
Spaghetti with vongole,
Panini which here, after two
Thousand years, is still fine Greek bread,
Stuffed veal, grilled birds, cold spinach,
Washed down with Lachryma Christi,
And finished with tortoni and
Coffee like a skyrocket,
Laced with grappa aruta.
In Italy, as in America,
A symptom of a good restaurant
Is a wall covered with photos
Of opera singers. At the
Next table is a party of
Drummers from Lombardy. They
Agree with us about Naples.
"Italy is like America
With its Negroes. But here the
Negroes are white. These starving
People are the finest in
Italy. Once they escape from
The slavery of the Church and learn
The meaning of freedom, they will
Free Italy, just like they did
Before. Garibaldi's Thousand
Will some day be paid back with millions

Of a New Italy." It's
A word's been used a long time,
Italia Nuova.

In America today
Sex as such is regrettable,
But it can be channelized
Into socially useful forms.
From birth there exists a host
Of special policemen, the Black
Hundreds of Democracy,
Pediatricians, social
Workers, psychiatric social
Workers, psychiatrists, child
Guidance clinics, vocational
Guidance clinics, marriage guidance
Clinics, psychoanalysts,
Counselors, and psychologists.
Like most policemen they are
Largely homosexual
Sadists, and are thoroughly
Quantified, passionate pseudo
Marxists and Freudians. Their
Job is to see that sexual
Relations are kept as much like
A visit to a painless
American dentist as possible.

From the Greeks to the Normans
Communal life was especially
Strong, but from then on Naples
Has been without a polity.
Since the beginning of the
Middle Ages, it has been
A piece of real estate bandied
About between dynastic
Cadets and by-blows. Only
Under the pagan Frederick
Did it enjoy a brief moment
Of civilization. Which shows

What one civilized man can do.
The Renaissance started with
His sculptors, his coins are as fine
As the Arethusa of
Syracuse or the Bactrian Kings.
Aquinas grew up in his court
In the company of Arab
Mystics, troubadours, and Kabbalists.
Murat denied the Emperor
And dickered with Metternich
And ended like Black Christophe.
The Pope filled the vacuum.
Naples never had a Nineteenth
Century. If you advocated
Kindness to animals you'd
Be a revolutionary.
But in the local dungeon,
Held incommunicado,
Is Italy's first war resister.
Angevin, Spaniard, Bourbon,
What survives under priestcraft,
Starvation, terror, ignorance,
Is the soul of a Greek polis.

In America today
All basic experience is
Looked on as a morbid condition,
An actual serious sickness.
There are doctors specializing
In each of them—being born,
Childhood, puberty, fucking,
Parenthood, vocation, growing
Old, and dying. These crises
Of life are the matter of
The sacraments in more normal
Societies—baptism,
Confirmation, marriage,
Orders, communion, unction—
Moments when life necessarily
Transcends any quantitative

Experience altogether—
Windows into reality.
In America they are
Given into the aseptic
Hands of medical specialists,
From obstetricians to
Geriatrists. This is a
Picture of a nation gone
Stark raving mad, in the grip
Of mutually homicidal
Paranoia. So it is
Fitting that its sacrament
Should be the atom bomb, the
Apotheosis of quantity.
The blazing mushroom cloud is
Just such a mystical vision
As one would expect of the
Managers of the du Pont
Industries and their enslaved
Physicists, of Mr. ——, who
Bears so fatal a resemblance
To the grinning monsters who
Are the heroes of the
Advertising pages.

Alchemy started as the
Craft of metals, ended in
Sex mysticism. Science
Started as a mystical
Doctrine of the pure atom,
Being as self subsistent,
Ended in catastrophe.

Against arithmetic man
There can be only vengeance.
A murder can be healed,
But vengeance is incurable.

We fill our rucksacks at a
Rôtisserie just like the ones

In Pompeii, with bread just like the
Pumice casts, and take the train
To the South. In our compartment
Is an aged widow who gives
Us a message for her sister
In San Francisco. She is
Travelling third class from Milan
To Palermo, erect on the
Board bench like a white hawk in
Black silk. Our wineskin from the
Pyrenees creates a sensation.
All the men cheer as we hold
It at arm's length and spurt the
Wine, usually, into our mouths.
Everybody takes a drink.
We figure they have decided
There are some good Americans.
Then we find out they think we're French.
We tell them we're Americans,
And then they do become friendly,
They were being cool before.

Paestum, the apex of the trip,
And the zenith of our years.

Helen's jewel, the Schethya,
The Taoist uncut block,
The stone of the alchemist,
The footstool of Elohim's throne,
Which they hurled into the Abyss,
On which stands the queen and sacred
Whore, Malkuth, the stone which served
Jacob for pillow and altar.

"And what is truth?" said Pilate,
"A,E,I,O,U—the spheres
Of the planets, the heavens'
Pentachord. A noir, E blanc,
I rouge, O bleu, U vert."

When in Japan, the goddess
Of the sun, attracted by
The obscene gestures of the flesh,
Came out from eclipse, she spoke
The first and oldest mystery,
"1, 2, 3, 4, 5, 6, 7,
8, 9, 10."

All things have a name.
Every mote in the sunlight has
A name, and the sunlight itself
Has a name, and the spirit who
Troubles the waters has a name.

As the Philosopher says,
"The Pythagoreans are
Of the opinion that the shapes
Of the Greek vase are reflections
Of the irrational numbers
Thought by the Pure Mind. On the
Other hand, the Epicureans
Hold them to be derived
From the curves of a girl's
Breasts and thighs and buttocks."

The doctrine of Signatures—
The law by which we must make
Use of things is written in
The law by which they were made.
It is graven upon each
As its unique character.
The forms of being are the
Rules of life.

The Smaragdine Tablet
Says, "That which is above is
Reflected in that which is below."

Paestum of the twice blooming
Roses, the sea god's honey-

Colored stone still strong against
The folly of the long decline
Of man. The snail climbs the Doric
Line, and the empty snail shell
Lies by the wild cyclamen.
The sandstone of the Roman
Road is marked with sun wrinkles
Of prehistoric beaches,
But no time at all has touched
The deep constant melodies
Of space as the columns swing
To the moving eye. The sea
Breathes like a drowsy woman.
The sun moves like a drowsy hand.
Poseidon's pillars have endured
All tempers of the sea and sun.
This is the order of the spheres,
The curve of the unwinding fern,
And the purple shell in the sea;
These are the spaces of the notes
Of every kind of music.
The world is made of number
And moved in order by love.
Mankind has risen to this point
And can only fall away,
As we can only turn homeward
Up Italy, through France, to life
Always pivoted on this place.

Sweet Anyte of Tegea—
"The children have put purple
Reins on you, he goat, and a
Bridle in your bearded mouth.
And they play at horse races
Round a temple where a god
Gazes on their childish joy."

Finally the few tourists go,
The German photographers, the
Bevy of seminarians,

And we are left alone. We eat
In the pronaos towards the sea.
Greek food, small white loaves, smoked cheese,
Pickled squid, black figs, and honey
And olive oil, the common food
Of Naples, still, for those who eat.
An ancient dog, Odysseus' dog,
Spawned before there were breeds of dogs,
Appears, begs, eats, and disappears—
The exoteric proxy of
The god. And we too grow drowsy with
White wine, tarry from the wineskin.
The blue and gold shafts interweave
Across our nodding eyes. The sea
Prepares to take the sun. We go
Into the naos, open to the
Sky and make love, where the sea god
And the sea goddess, wet with sperm,
Coupled in the incense filled dark,
As the singing rose and was still.

Mist comes with the sunset. (The Yanks
Killed the mosquitoes.) Long lines of
Umber buffalo, their backs a
Rippling congruence, as in the
Paintings of Krishna, file across
The brilliant green sea meadows,
Under banners of white mist.
The fires of the bivouacs of
Spartacus twinkle in the hills.
Our train comes with the first stars.
Venus over the wine dark sea.

All the way back the train fills
And fills up, and fills again,
With girls from the fish canneries,
And girls from the lace factories,
And girls from the fields, who have been
Working twelve hours for nothing,
Or at the best a few pennies.

They laugh and sing, all the way
Back to Naples, like broad bottomed,
Deep bosomed angels, wet with sweat.

Only in a secret place
May human love perfect itself.

In the mountains above Bologna
A ropewalk, two lean faced, copper
Skinned men, who tread like cats,
Spinning hemp. "Illyrians,"
Strabo called them Pelasgoi,
Who were here before Etruscan,
Greek, Celt, Roman, or Goth. A loud
Crowd of peasants swarming bees.
All the hundred armies passed
This way, but the peasants stayed.

The twilight asked the dark, "Why
Do you move away from me?" "I do
Not move myself. I am cast by
A body which I cannot
See, and which made me, and moves
Me, according to the laws of
Opacity and movement."

The shadows of the towers
Of Bologna move on the
Walls of the cramped, noisy square,
Red gnomons of history.
Ruskin called them Jove's spent thunder
Bolts. Carducci wrote his best poem
About them, a dialogue of
The long betrayal of Italy
By the Evil Twins, Church and Empire.

You go to Ferrara for
Lasagne verde. The art is
Rigid as the Palazzo

Diamante, there is just the
Moated Este castle and the
Food, but the food is worth it.

The sun enters the second
Moon of Autumn. The dove turns
To a hawk. Dew becomes hoarfrost.

Ravenna, October, night,
The Pleiades are rising
Over Dante's tomb with its
Always burning, blood-red lamp.
On the walls of the loggia,
Between the shadows of the
Columns and the curves of the
Arches, the Autumn wind sways the
Shadows of palm and laurel leaves.
Theodoric's tomb in the rain,
The monolith split by a bomb.
I ask about the ruined fort
Nearby. "Ah, signore, the Inglesi,
They hate and envy Italia."
Doubtless true, but in this case,
No Inglese later than
Hawkwood. There is no question
The English rankled under
Their defeat by an army
Which couldn't handle the Greeks,
So they did as much damage as
Possible once the Pope and
Giannini presented them
With a defenseless ally.
The average Italian is
Convinced they are to blame for the
Condition of the Roman Forum.
The Communists control the town,
And it is a concentration
Point for the Pope and the USA.
The whole place broods under a

Fog of deadlocked hostility,
A dry hate as barbarous
As Mexico. Still, nobody
Hates Americans, they are
Children, good hearted, but misled,
By the Pope and the Inglesi.
Stalin's smartest move was to
Inveigle America
Into an alliance with
A power which is not only
Without divisions, but which
Can never, founded firmly as
It is on biological
Nonsense, do anything but fail.

We peek in the windows of
The Albergo Commercio.
The walls are covered with photos
Of opera singers. This is it.
Our room with its immense oaken
Letto matrimoniale
Is barren and noble. The food—
The food is beyond question
The best I have ever eaten
Cooked by an Occidental.
It is simple enough. The cook
Is an old woman. Usually
I loathe female cooking, but she
Makes magic over it. The cold
Green beans are just cold green beans,
The sliced eggplant has only
Been dipped in oil and garlic
And broiled, the steamed fish is just steamed,
The veal is the same national
Animal of Italy,
The guinea hen is baked, the birds
Are spitted and broiled. Nothing else.
It seems to be, as in the best
Chinese cooking, a matter
Of absolute accuracy

In timing and flavoring.
Impossible to believe,
She can turn out a better
Lasagne verde than can be
Found publicly in Ferrara.

It is unfortunately
The case, that the world in which
We live is dominated
By two collectivities
Whose whole force is exerted
To depersonalize and
Quantify persons—the State
And the Capitalist System.
If a person is that which
By definition can never
Be added to anything else,
The State is precisely the
Mechanism by which persons
Are reduced to integers.
The State exists to add and
Subtract, divide and multiply
Population units. Its
Components have no more and
No less reality than the
Mathematics of the battlefield.
Similarly, Capitalism
Views all existence in the form
Of commodities. Nothing
Is valuable except to
The extent it will bring a
Profit on the market. Again,
The human being is reduced
To a special commodity,
Labor power, his potential
To make other commodities.
Labor power on the market,
Firepower on the battlefield,
It is all one, merely two
Aspects of the same monster.

The parliaments of the State
Are only highly ritualized
Capitalist market places.
The battlefield is only
The most advanced form of trade.

The equities of the State
Are only devices for
Postponing the decisions
Of violence to a more
Opportune moment. The ballot
Is a paper substitute
For the billy, the bullet,
And the bayonet.

McTaggart:
"Better worship a crocodile
Which being a sentient being
Has some value, than the State, which,
Being an instrument, has none.
As well worship a sewer pipe,
Which may have considerable
Instrumental value."

The times come round, once more all
Our hearts are breaking as the world
Drowns in a marsh of blood and fire.

How poor they were in the last hours.
What a little thing the tomb
Of Galla Placida is.
An ordinary mechanic
In Los Angeles could contract
For a small monthly payment, and
Get as good a job when he died.
San Vitale's dimensions
Are not marked on the floor of
St. Peter's. The mosaicist
Of the Twenty-third Psalm was
Hardly Christian. You can see

Justinian's dissipated
Face any day at the Stork Club
Or on the Place Vendôme, and the
Exophthalmic, sex-crazed eyes of
Theodora glare through the smoke
Of every Harry's Bar
Around the world and wink across
The aisle in every airliner.
I hate to seem fashionable, but
I guess this is the art I like
Best in all of Italy.
Since the Greeks nobody knew
Better how to put together
The simplest forms and make the most
Complex harmonies—second hand
Columns, red bricks, and bits of
Colored stone and gilded glass.
Poor Richardson. They tried hard
To make Chicago look like this.

Every collectivity
Is opposed to community.
As Capitalism and the
State have become identical,
All existence assumes the
Character of a vast
Conspiracy to quantify
The individual and
Convince him that all other
Seeming persons are actually
Already successfully
And happily quantified,
And that all human relations
Are quantitative, commodity
Relationships. This means murder.
Every minute, in a million
Ways, the society in which
You live is trying to murder
You. War is the health of the State?
War against its own members.

And with the falling rate of
Profit, all commodities,
Including you, as a unit
Of labor power, become
War matériel, nothing more.

"A golden book, worthy of
The leisure of Plato or Tully."
I am older than Boethius,
Executed age forty-three.
"Whatever, therefore, comprehends
And possesses the whole fullness
Of unlimited life at once,
Where nothing future is lacking
And none of the past flows away,
May be truly called eternal."
Here the last philosopher died,
In contemplation, "in the last
Gloomy hours of Theodoric."
And with the two, king and martyr,
Italy's last chance of life.
Nobody won but the Pope.
From this base Justinian's
Cuckold and eunuch accomplished
The decline and fall of the
Roman Empire in two fell swoops.
All in the name of the unity
Of the Divine Nature. I have
Always wondered about him. Did
It give Justinian a special
Thrill to screw a Monophysite?
Here Maximian wrote his
Elegies of impotence,
Of the tedium and horror
Of the end of the world.
I like to fancy that the
Bitter face of the Maximian
In the mosaic is his.
Here Dante died and Byron
Lusted and played cicisbeo.

Here the Risorgimento
And the Papacy stabbed at
Each other in secret. Now,
Every night in the Piazza
A loudspeaker blares, the voice, smooth
As a preacher's prick in a calf's arse,
Dripping with lachrymose evil,
Of a Passionist missioner.
On alternate weekends the Church
And the Communists march through the
Streets with their respective idols.

I see the water, I see
The fire, the air, and the earth,
And all their mixtures, come to
Decay and last but little.

Be still and let the years revolve.

There would seem to be some in whom
The potential personality
Of others is sacrificed
To the ever diminishing
Realization of the self,
Still considered in terms of
Possibility and consequence.
This is evil, the total
Distortion of the end of life.
All that we know of life is love,
All that we know of the world
Of happenings is that it is
Shot through and through with offers
Of love. What we realize
In the beloved is the
Growing reality of
All the others. The sacrifice
Of millions of human beings
Or one human being, for
The most sublime goals, is
A defeat of being itself.

It is obvious that the Jews
Or the Ukrainian peasants,
Or the Chinese middle class,
Cannot be exterminated
To advance even the most
Glorious future society,
Without destroying the inner
Reality, the persons, of
Their altruistic murderers.
But the universe of persons
Cannot in any way be
Manipulated as a
Condition of community,
Of love. The community
Is always there, beyond cause
And effect, or time and space,
And only contingencies
May be manipulated.
The politician works in
The materials of his
Own destruction—by definition.

I pay a visit to ————.
When she opens the door, she says,
"Don't blame me, they're just using
The place." All the American
Consuls in Italy, but one,
And their wives, are having a
Party. The men all look like
Gas station attendants, their wives,
Like their wives, except the one wife
Whose husband is away. She is
Très civilisée, oh, so
Continental, black haired,
Haggard, glare eyed, and brave, brave,
And oh, so witty. ———— says,
"He was here this spring, driving
Mrs. Crosby to Paris."
The brave one says, "Bing? Oh! Bing! Bing!
You had an affair with Bing?

I have always wanted Bing,
Ravenously, ever since
I saw that gorgeous *Boys Town*."
This goes on without the least
Pause, all evening; except when
It gets extra loud, it is
Possible to ignore it.
Sometimes she is pretty funny.
They suspect the fact that I am
Some highbrow friend of————'s and
All try to talk big. I find
That few of them speak Italian,
And that the principal source
Of diplomatic information
Seems to be their wives' servants.
As I listen, it occurs to
Me that most of Gertrude Stein is
This stuff, slightly dissociated,
And this is the class she spoke for.
They leave, but in a minute
Back they come. The brave one is
Raging. "Come with me. Come with me.
Protect me from them. They tried
To put me in a traghetto
That wasn't there, and besides
The man was drunk." We wearily
Go with them. Somehow I am
Left to pay the traghettatore,
To whom I whisper, "Viva
Il Pian' Marshall." "Si, si, dronk
Bambini." As I rejoin them
In the midst of freezing fog,
A consul says, "Do you play bridge?"
"Not any more than I can help."
"But you can?" "Yes." Instantly, I am
Dealt a card. The deal goes round
And the bidding starts. We are
Walking through a narrow lane
Almost invisible to
Each other in the blowing fog.

"Two hearts." "Three spades."
"Three hearts." My turn—
Fortunately we have reached
The door of the Danieli.
"Sorry," I say, "I must go on."
The brave one screams, "But you aren't
Coming in? You won't play bridge?"
"No." "But it's you, you, I want.
We'll play like madmen. We'll drink
Gallons and gallons of absinthe,
I'll trump your aces all night long,
Till the dawn comes up like thunder,
From the Lido 'cross the bay."
I go home. It isn't funny.
It will be hard to forget
That useless body and those
Nerve wracked, empty eyes.

The vulture is only female
And fertilized by the wind.
Viva videns vivo
Sepiliri viscera busto.

Neurosis develops first
In the vegetative system.
Man, when he fails as a man,
Dies first as a plant.
The divorce at Cana where
The wine turned into water.
Insanity is the crippling
Of the organ of reciprocity.

The snake bodied, tortoise beaked
Clutch footed Eumenides.

Tara, the Counter Buddha,
Is a supremely beautiful
Courtesan, born in a time
When history has filled its cup

With chaos and tragedy.
As the world is transfigured
By the Divine Couple at
Its apogee, so in the
Depth of its declension it is
Returned and redeemed by the
Coupling of the warrior and
The whore, the beggar and the queen.
The madman and beggar, and
The whore are sperm cell and egg
By which one society
Passes to another. Hence
The State in our time has turned
On them with special savagery.

Jealousy is a kind of
Murder, murder is a kind of
Jealousy. The end of life
Is the full communion of
Lovers, the only absolute.
There is little doubt but what
There exist persons who view
The relation with others
And with the beloved as
Restrictive and acquisitive.
This is what evil is, the
Translation of the terms of
Illusion into the world
Of reality. What this
Means, of course, is that the real
Is thereby so much impoverished.
When this is the typical
Activity of the person,
We are safe in ascribing
Evil motives. The person
Is growing less and less
And life is being narrowed.
It is perhaps possible
That in the community

Of persons which is reality
The activity of the members
Goes both ways, as obviously
It does in man's history.

We sit above the rain-flooded
Piazza San Marco in a
Workers' club and talk to two
Young anarchist leaders. They ask
Me about California.
"Do I know Lily La Rue?"
"Oh yes, she gave a lot of
Money to the cotton strikers."
"La Verne De Vere?" "Oh yes, she sang
At an entertainment for Spain."
"Billy McAgy?" "Very well.
His father was a Wobbly,
Once he spoke for Tom Mooney
And filled the auditorium."
I notice their puzzled faces.
We are talking at cross purposes.
The Grapes of Wrath, is it true?
"One eighth true; in the book, one man
Is killed, actually there were eight."
"Then the American workers
Are fighters?" "Yes, they fought for
What they got. Now they have got it."
I ask them about the workers
In Venice. Like the middle class
Everywhere, they talk about the
Only workers they know—servants.
"In Venice, the workers are all
Gondoliers, or porters, or
Waiters, or hotel employees."
"Between Venice and Padova
Are miles and miles of the finest
Docks in Europe, all idle.
What about them?" On this subject
They have no information.

There are reasons for and against
Assuming that being is
In its nature progressive.
If being is essentially
Active, action would seem to
Imply a positive and
Negative, even beyond time.
Just as some persons move deeper
Into the plenum of the
Community of love, so
Others may be moving, or
All or some may move at times,
Towards the isolation of
The ego, not being, hate,
Ultimate atomization.

It is a great art in the
World, to know how to sell wind.
A meeting in a Renaissance
Palazzo to reunite the
Shattered Socialist Party.
Silone talks for an hour
All about Democracy.
Not a word about the problems
Of this country which is bleeding
To death. Not a word about
The Pope. It sounds like an
Enormously expanded
Luce editorial, but
Chambers was a better writer—
So much less emotional.
The Stalinists always measure
The success of their meetings
By the number of Negroes,
Youth, and women they bring out.
Here are five hundred gabardined
Employees and petty bourgeois,
No Sicilians or Trentinos,
One worker, a gondolier,

Who paces the floor and leaves early,
Five women, two aging copies
Of Beatrice Webb, and three housewives
With their husbands, who go to sleep.
As poor old Trotsky used to say,
"Power lies in the streets and
No one knows how to pick it up."

It is even possible
That the movement is circular,
That persons flow from pole to pole.
This was Boehme's belief and it
Has colored all German thought.
Even their most ambitious
Systems of morality,
Nietzsche's, for instance, seemed robbed of
Meaning by its application.
Its truth may at least be doubted.
The satisfactions of the
Community of lovers
Are inexhaustible and
The lure of love of person
For person so great that it
Seems likely that all persons
Are caught up eventually
In the full community of
Love or pass out of existence.
Of course this discussion is
Haunted by the terms of space
And time, possibility
And consequence. Actually
The community of lovers
Is always there. It grows, not
In time, like a vine on a rod,
But in compass and intensity,
State within state, like the wave
Motion of ripples from a stone,
If it moved both in and out
At once. The physical evils
Of pain and waste and loss are

Easily dismissed. Most thinkers
Have evaded the problem
By identifying them with
The problem of moral evil.
Pain, waste, and loss are inherent
In the world of contingency.
Death, sickness, suffering may
Fill us with an agony of
Compassion when we witness them
In others, and when they occur
To ourselves, move us but little.
It is love makes us suffer with
The poor doped babies of Naples,
They do not know they suffer.
As for ourselves in this world
Of acquiring and losing—we
Will die, probably painfully,
And lose all of it at once.
Moral evil, the denial,
Betrayal, or debauching
Of love is another matter.
The evil person, assuming
His existence, remains the
Mystery he has always been.
But one should never forget,
He appears only in the
Context of a collectivity,
And the person is real
Only in community.

We walk thousands of miles and look
At acres of Tintorettos.
We spend days in the Scuola
San Rocco. We do not miss a church.
At last in this floating city
We become disembodied.
The law of gravity dies out.
All solids interpenetrate.
All space is cobwebbed and netted.
The mind is entirely possessed

By the breathing vortex of
Creation itself. Fiat!
It is like nitrous oxide, but
Nitrous oxide with a meaning
That lasts after it is over.
"In St. Hildegarde of Bingen
The identification
Of idioretinal
Disturbances with the mystic
Light is unmistakable."
What happens when a culture
Peters out? How can these people
Live under a sky of the thought
Of "the mightiest mind that
Ever applied itself to painting"
And be so ordinary?
We find out. After a while
We are exhausted. Titian
Is so sane and solid, the flesh
And smoke and dark, and the orange flame
That rings like a somber bell
In his San Lorenzo seem more
Wise as well as more real. His
"Presentation" is less tricky
As well as a profounder judgment.
So we come back, one by one,
To the others, Bellini's
Mysterious, transcendent flesh,
Carpaccio's russet cube of dream,
Indecipherable Giorgione,
Veronese, Marlowe in paint,
And Tiepolo, so cultured,
And so dreadfully obscene.
When it dawns on me what St. Lucy
Is really up to, even I
Blush. We discover all sorts
Of things, for instance, that the
Guardi ceilings in the Ca'
Rezzonico are in pastel.

And every day I stop and look
At the four last rulers of Rome,
Clutching each other in fear.

And every day we eat well,
In this city of foul cuisine,
In the Casa Paganelli,
The cheapest hotel in town,
And we have real breakfasts with good
Caffè latte and fresh pastry
By the Tre Ponti and the Greek Church.
These are good places to know—
Venice is a tourist trap,
The first and greatest in the world.
Mostly we eat lunch on the street.
We suck jacknife clams still
Wiggling, walk along muzzling
Great dripping kakis, munch rotten
Medlars in churches and
Pickled polpi in palazzi.
All the Venetians have to do
Is put food on a stove to spoil it.
But the wines are wonderful,
Valpolicella, Bardolino,
And the small wines of Trentino.

All too often where we might,
By seeking, find a person,
We are content to hang a
Specter that haunts ourselves.
The triangle of consequence,
Result, action, and appetite,
Appetite, action, and result,
Spins like the coat of arms of the
Isle of Man, until it erupts
Into a kind of false being,
The ghost or demon of the deed.
The *Tale of Genji* is the
Story of generations

Of beauty destroyed by a
Devil which sprang from a moment
Of wrath and jealousy, and whose
Power grew for years until
It was dissolved by one pure act
Of gracious, casual compassion.

If we cannot be assured
That any human being
Or group of human beings
Is any more real than any
Of the other occasions of
The world, we cannot literally
Love our neighbor as ourselves,
Because love is reciprocal,
And in the majority
Of our encounters with our
Neighbors, they show no signs of
Wishing to transcend the thingness
They share with all impersonal
Experience, and enter
Into any personal, let
Alone a love relationship.
All we can do is to try
To love one another, and through
The beloved to love all
She loves, and to keep ourselves
Open to the love of others.

A day with the Giottos in
Padova, the best thing is the
Donkey. The Mantegnas were bombed.
Vicenza for Palladio,
And the Villa Valmarana,
And then on to Verona.
San Zeno and the arena,
And then lunch with Mardersteig.
No better printer anywhere,
One of those perfect craftsmen

In whom absolute devotion
And respect for a medium
Has produced a state of being
Which can only be called saintly,
A personality like a
Work of art, a true state of grace.
We both think of the portrait of
Luca Pacioli in Naples.
Autumn planting in Lombardy,
As the sower walks along
A puff of dark dust flies from
His hand and floats away with
Each cast. The grain is mixed with soil.

Sirmio, a dark blue grey sky
Above the grey blue lake, the sun
Breaking through the mountains at the
Far end, its light a pale, soft orange;
Dull red leaves on the hillsides,
Bright yellow poplars on the shores;
Everything else wet brown, dusky
Blue, and chalky white. Dürer
Painted his watercolors here,
And here Tiepolo found those
Terribly civilized color chords.
Catullus certainly picked
A lovely spot for himself.
I will never do as well.
But I have never been the lover
Of "the most depraved daughter
Of the Claudian line," either.

Milano, a big show of
Public Health work in Italy.
Very impressive, perfect
Techniques, as good as the States.
Behind these montages and
Movies are thousands of poorly
Paid, hard working idealists,

Many of them Americans.
The statistics of what they've done
Are very impressive, too,
Until you read the statistics
Of the real situation.
You can plug dikes with a finger,
But you can't plug a tidal wave.

Normally one would assume
That what appears as a group
Of human beings would be
An aspect of persons in
A community of love.
Unfortunately mankind
Appears collectively almost
Always as an instrumentality
Of the State, as malignant,
If not openly murderous.
I have never encountered
Even good will in any
Collectivity. I know of
No association of men
Which cannot be demonstrated
To have been, ultimately,
Organized for purposes
Of coercion and mutual
Destruction. By far the worst
Are the putative communal
And benevolent gangsters.
Lawrence pointed out long ago
That the most malignant form
Of hate is benevolence.
Social frightfulness has increased
In exact proportion to
Humanitarianism.
In the nation of the atom
Bomb, dentists inject narcotics
Before they clean your teeth. The
Society of Friends has the
Honor of having introduced

The concentration camp into
America, of course under
Very humane auspices.

Milanese food is world famous,
But when I want French food, I'll take
It straight without tomato sauce.
However, Milano has the
World's best snails, cared for better
Than most Italian babies and
Fed on vine leaves and polenta.

The Cathedral—why on earth
Did they want to try to build
A thing like that in Italy?
But Sant' Ambrogio, that is a
Different matter, its Milanese
Barn roof filled with flying golden
Geometry. And the Cena—
Leonardo has always
Annoyed me, he seems like a
Renaissance Marcel Duchamp,
And Freud was certainly right
About that sickening St. John.
But once in his life he was both
Transfigured and accomplished.
Fresh from the Scuola San Rocco,
And the Stanze of Raphael,
This tattered cloud of color,
Filled with the forms of gods and
Every tragedy of man,
Beggars all Italian painting.
We look at it all day long.
Just before the light goes, a group
Of schoolgirls comes in. They all stand
At the back and listen to their
Nun. Except one little blonde girl,
About twelve, with a face of
Untempered sensibility,
Who advances slowly, hands

Folded, lips parted, eyes rapt away.
We turn aside, as though we had
Pried on the vision of a saint.
I say to Marthe, "I would
Give anything in the world to
Have a daughter like that." Our
Daughter is already alive.
The next day we leave Italy.

To match the scarlet of the
Autumn leaves, the red sunlight
Glitters on the flowing stream.
Lago Maggiore, blue black
And grey with bands of silver.
Deep Autumn, the orange fruit
And olive grey bare branches
Of the kakis silhouetted
In dark air. And at the last
Italy only a dimness
And vastness of gold filled fog
Behind us in the narrow mountains.

There are more fallen leaves than I
Ever saw growing on the trees.

IV

Over Switzerland broods the
Anal ghost of Karl Barth's church
Of spiritual masochism,
Up to date religion for the
Inmates of a world in barbed wire,
And the miasma of Jung's
Health resort occultism,
For the bored wives of the screws.
Switzerland is the world's worst
Country—Kansas stood on end.

A real religion is not
Believed in, it is practiced.
Julian was not the reviver
Of paganism, but the
Unsuccessful founder of
A sect. So his competitors,
The Christians, except where they
Have been overcome by the
Ancient cults they tolerated,
Began as, and remain late
Hellenistic sectarians.
Neither Augustine nor Karl Barth
Are religious men. They are
Emotionally unstable
Philosophers. The savage fills
The gap between technology
And environment with
Projections of himself.
If he is successful he is
Unaware of the gap until
Confronted with a sewing machine.

The World Soul, the point where the
Sun's path crosses the ecliptic,
Moves through the constellations,
Slow as the waste of mountains
In the midst of falling water.
The Zodiac revolves like
A waterwheel of which the
Planets are the buckets and
Gathers light generated
By contemplation and pours
It into the lamps of the world,
The sun and moon. The world passes
Like a white pony which flashes
Past a gap in a hedge.

The year
6666
The rainbow will shine like a bride,

Adorned for the bed of her spouse.
A star will rise in the east and
Swallow seven stars in the north.
A star will appear at the Pole.
It will shine for seventy days.
It will have seventy stars.
Rome will fall into ruins.
The celestial   ו   will raise up
The terrestrial   ה   into the
Bliss of sexual union.

Love and do what you will.
Love slays what we have been,
That we may be what we were not.

Dans l'automne vaine
Les feuilles tombent
Des kakis, où les singes
S'agrippent dans leurs
Fourrures ahuries.

Paris at midnight, colder
Than a witch's tit. We cower
In our Italian clothes and hunt
A cab. A little jumping wisp
Of a man with bright Celtic eyes
Escorts us to the last cab
That won the battle of the Marne.
The porter, covered with luggage,
Is so drunk he can't see, and must
Be led like a dizzy camel.
"Votre voiture va plus?" "Oui, oui,
M'sieu, madame. Elle marche doucement
Avec les années de la sagesse."
Spurred, she explodes and shakes herself,
And starts off with only one lamp,
Peering weakly through the rain.
"Ah, la bonne auto! Elle a été
La bonne, et la camarade très
Fidéle!" Entering Boulevard
St. Germain, a traffic cop

Whistles. She rears and quivers
And shuts her eye and dies.
The cop comes over, soaked with rain.
"Vous n'avez pas la lumière."
"Ah, mais oui, je n'ai qu'une, mais
Très efficace, toutes les fois
Qu'elle va, alors, elle éclaire!"
"J' comprends. C'est pour ça que j'vous ai arrêté.
Changez la lumière active
A la gauche. Faites sûr que ça
S'allume avant de repartir"
This is no enemy of the people.
He presses his lips and goes away.
The cabby changes the lamps.
Nothing happens. He tinkers with
The dashboard. Nothing happens.
He jumps out again and gently
Pats the light. It lights.
There is no lens and it lights up
His face, streaming with rain, suffused
With the great joy of relief
From a terrible fear. "M'sieu,
Madame, je vous disais, n'est-ce pas,
Qu'elle était la bonne camarade?"
All the pathos and anguish
And heroism of the French
Working class hits us in the face
Like a bludgeon. "Nous ne sommes
Rien, soyons tout!" But when?
When? When? In the bitter rain
On the Boulevard St. Germain?

Edgar Quinet—not a whore out
In the storm. Our reservations
Have been forgotten. Two o'clock
Before we find a narrow bed,
And furiously make love,
To assure ourselves our blood
Still circulates. In the dark hall
Under a one watt lamp, a sign—

LE SILENCE
DE CHACUN
ASSURE
LE REPOS
DE TOUS

When they caught
Vaillant trying to blow the
Chambre to smithereens, the
Judge said, "But think of all the
Innocent people you would
Have killed." He replied, "There are
No innocent bourgeois."

We have
Fed you all for a thousand years
And you hail us still unfed.

Anyone in France with an
Income of over sixty dollars
A month is a rascal, and this
Includes existentialists,
Poets, artists, Communists,
All colors of labor fakers,
From anarchist to royalist.
They all piss through the same quill.
Ye are many, they are few.

There are only two classes,
Members of communities,
Members of collectivities,
And they have nothing in common.
Mankind will sink only deeper
Into mutual murder,
As long as collectivity
Robs them of their persons, starves
And dehumanizes them,
Deranges their desires, crazes
Them with insane appetites
Instead of the satisfactions

230

Of mutual love, provides them
With commodities which turn
To guns in their hands and bullets
In their bowels, and leaves them
Finally, perfect, abstract
Integers, anonymous white
X's in battlefield graveyards.

Between these two classes a
Struggle must go on until
Mankind is exterminated,
Or all abstract, coercive
Collectivities are destroyed,
And the satisfaction of
Human needs becomes a minor
Part of the fulfillment of
Personal desire, in a
Community of love.

La Nuit de la Libertaire
At the Mutualité.
An endless entertainment,
All the best raconteurs and
Singers of Paris donate
Their services, the bitter
Humor and passion of the
Dispossessed, gone from the States
With the old tramp carnivals
I followed once in Arkansas,
The voice of the Buttes Chaumont,
The true blague of Pig Alley.
At the end, mass chants by the
Auberge Jeunesse Laïque, *Spain*
Will Rise Again, Our Martyrs.
One by one, boys and girls step out
And sing a name. I am moved
As the foreign names ring out,
And then, unprepared, I hear,
"Parsons, Frank Little, Joe Hill,
Wesley Everest, Sacco,

Vanzetti." I weep like a baby.
Afterwards, when the dancing
Begins, we discover the cadres
In double breasted gabardines,
Sitting in a side room at a
Long table, solemnly sipping
Beer, like the Central Committee
In a Pudovkin movie.
They are horrified when we
Jitterbug with the young comrades.
No hope there. But along the
Beautiful rivers of France,
And in the mountains, next summer
Boys and girls will be making love,
And singing the songs of Joe Hill
In their own language. "Song on his
Lips he came, song on his lips he
Went. This be the burden of his
Refrain, soldier of discontent."
Hideux dans leur apothéose,
Les rois de la mine et du rail
Ont-ils jamais fait autre chose
Que dévaliser le travail?
Combien de nos chairs se repaissent!
Mais si les corbeaux, les vautours,
Un de ces matins, disparaissent,
Le soleil brillera toujours!

No collectivity against
Collectivities can function
To restore community.
You cannot creep from quantity
To quality. Today the world is full
Of the vendors of well policed
Utopias, preachers of
Progress by mass arithmetic.
They are all liars, knowingly
Using the language of being
To sweeten the poison of
Death. Never has the last circle

Of Dante's Hell been so crowded.
While there is a lower class,
I am in it. While there is
A criminal element,
I am of it. Where there is
A soul in jail, I am not free.

In the Italian museums
The paintings look like very
Expensive treasures, but still
Works of art; elsewhere in Europe
They look like loot; in England
Like badges of Empire and class
Distinction, collective Orders
Of Merit; in the United
States they look like tastefully
Chosen, beautifully shown
Merchandise. French painting
Never de-provincialized
Itself. Most of it is sterile
And concocted. Poussin—the
Darling of the aesthetes who think
Copland sounds like Bach.
LeSueur, at once rigid and soft,
But in the Mass of St. Martin,
Uncanny as Easter Island.
The Nains, as academic
And Italianate as the Blue
And Pink Picassos which copy
Them. The Nineteenth Century
Largely the private conversation,
The symbols of a special
Antibourgeois way of life,
Of a secret revolutionary
Society. The Twentieth
A horrible collection
Of gadgets and infernal
Machines. Had Seurat lived things might
Have been different. What have you?
The boudoir painters, certainly

As good as Tiepolo, but
With less scale and no arrogance;
Lorrain, a sentimental
Peasant, touched with the over-
Ripe infantilism you
Think of with Richard Jefferies;
David, a pompous bureaucrat,
Except for little Val d'Ognes,
But I doubt if he painted her;
Ingres, an inflated lapidary;
Courbet and Delacroix, the
Only French painters who ever
Seriously tried to be
Major artists, one corrupted
By Haldeman-Julius, the
Other full of fustian, but as
Gide replied, "Hugo. Hélas!"
Even the failure in Saint
Sulpice has a kind of
Renaissance arrogance and might
Well be hanging in Italy.
The "French Moderns" are aged men.
Actually contemporary
Painting is awful past belief—
With the exception of Tal-Coat,
Who is a man in his forties.
The growing point of painting
Today has moved to Seattle.

Americans who worship
Richardson despise Abadie.
Although it is the symbol
Of Neo-Catholicism
And the Black Terror after
The Commune, still, Sacré Coeur
Is equalled by few churches in
Paris, and no archaistic
Churches elsewhere. Trinity
May be in better taste, but

It was so patently built
For Boston consumption.
St. Vincent Ferrer looks like
Gothic by Kohler of Kohler.
Liverpool is the tomb of
An Empire's hypocrisy.
"Functionalist churches" are
For people who have forgotten
The very meaning of a sect,
Let alone a religion.
Sante Cécile in Albi was
Another "cry of triumph
Over the Wall of the Communards."
Why shouldn't the ruling class
Be best when celebrating
Its most characteristic
Activity, mass murder?

There is a false impression
Abroad that American
Poetry has given up
The working class as a bad
Proposition and taken to
Form. This should be corrected.

Wine, women, and song,
Whiskey, pin-ups, and laxatives,
All the world raises hell about
Essenin and Mayakofsky.
Twenty-three poets of "anthology
Rank" have committed suicide
In the USA since 1900.
It is by far the commonest
Form of death amongst poets.
I am far better aware of
The evils of Stalinism
Than you are, you ex-Trotskyite
Warmonger. But it won't get you
Anywhere to tell me I should

Welcome the beast who devours me
Just because a bigger lion
Is eating somebody else on
The other side of the arena.

Love and lowliness and
Loyalty, these shall be
Lords in the land, truth to save.
For the world has lost his youth
And the times begin to wax old.

Léontine gives us a farewell.
"M. Kennet', un poète
Prolétarien, et sa femme,
Marthe, une jeune philosophe."
The tiny room is packed with guests;
A fat Italian sculptor who
Looks like a ragged, dying Wilde,
Epilepsy destroyed his hand,
Now he makes casts for the Louvre;
His silent, fat, Bretonne peasant wife;
A little wiry garagist,
Red faced, bright eyed, three times
Given up for dead with consumption,
Three years in concentration camps;
A Bretonne ex-seamstress who makes
Periodic trips to Belgium,
Where a girl can still find money;
Two neighbors, haggard young housewives,
Who eat and drink but hardly speak;
Léontine's first lover, an old
Shepherd from the Breton highlands,
With cheeks of purple morocco,
And eyes like a benevolent
Eagle. A wonderful dinner;
A pâté truffé; a brochet
Au beurre blanc; a bardatte,
The wild hare and woodcocks snared
By the shepherd; peas in cream;
Roast beef with a gravy of

Buckwheat flour, cream, and plums;
Choufleur farci; and a farsac'h,
The plum pudding of Brittany.
I bring the wine, Pelure d'oignon,
(Just like in America,
The girls prefer rosé) and a
Bottle of Calvados. They admire
Marthe's dress. "From a couturière?"
"Certainly not, I made it myself."
The atmosphere perceptibly
Lightens. Everybody eats, drinks,
Tells stories, sings songs, recites
Poetry. Over the coffee
The garagist cuts loose. His
Repertory is formidable.
"La Poule qu'était batie trop étroite,"
"Toute la nuit sur la Tour Eiffel,"
"L'Hirondelle avec les hémorroïdes sèches,"
(Hirondelles are bicycle cops),
And especially for the shepherd,
"Pompadour, ma belle angèle."
Léontine says, "He writes them all
Himself." I tell a story with
The punch line, "Ci-gît. Personne.
Son père utilise les
Produits Michelin." Great uproar.
The French all think their invention
Hilariously funny.
The shepherd is rather aloof
Until I tell him that once
I worked sheep, when I was a
Forest ranger in the Far West.
We get into a long discussion
Of sheepherding. I draw pictures
Of pack saddles, herders' wagons,
Tie a diamond hitch around his
Fingers. He is in ecstasy.
"La même, la même chose. Formidable.
Très ingénieuse." He wants to leave
For Nevada on the instant.

"C'est très simple," I say,
"Ecrivez une lettre au
Senator McCarran, et
Il vous fera venir outre-mer
Par avion; alors, vous
Gagnerez trois cents dollars par mois
Dès que vous signerez." "Impossible!"
"Impossible, mais c'est vrai." "Incroyable!"
The eagle's face gets a little
Foolish with shock. Léontine says,
"C'est absurde. L'Amérique vous
Tuerait. En France tu es
Un pauvre des pauvres, mais tu
As la bonne vie. Aux Etats-Unis,
Tu serais seul, dans le désert
Avec des milliards de moutons,
Et les loups de la prairie,
Les très sauvages coyotes,
Les ours de la montagne,
Les grizzlys féroces, les rattle
Snakes, et les sournois Peaux-Rouges."
"Je n'ai pas peur. Dans les
Pyrénées une fois . . ." "Tu n'avais pas
Peur, mais tu es vieux. Quand
Etais-tu dans les Pyrénées?
Pendant la Grande Guerre. M'sieu
Kennet' dit que tu conduirais
Les grands troupeaux à travers des
Milliers d'hectares. C'est la
Vitesse américaine dans les
Déserts. Et quand tu terminerais
Le travail, puis, quoi? Pas de
Léontine. Pas de Montparnasse.
Rien que le cowtown, les cowboys,
Le jukebox, le pinball, le whiskey.
Vous ne savez pas jouer au poker."
The old wisdom comes back in his
Face and he smiles his sly smile.
"L'illusion d'un moment,
Ma chérie, ce n'est qu'un cauchemar.

Je n'irai pas à moins que
Tu n'y ailles aussi. Tu
Pourrais être une dancing-girl
Parmi les cowboys et les Peaux-Rouges."
The garagist raises his glass,
And says, "Ki Yi Yippee Yi Yi!"
He has come back from his own room,
Bringing a sheaf of drawings, and
A box of beautiful models.
As he shows them to me his face
Lights with exaltation, and his
Movements grow entranced and still
More quick. I am dumfounded.
He has managed to discover
A fundamentally new
Application of a double
Torsion. I cannot tell through his
Excited language if he is
Aware of this or not.
He has perfect models of a
Stabilizer for the latest
Ford, a coupling for heavy trailers,
A gimmick for jet airplanes
I do not quite understand,
And last—"I hoped this at least
Could be sold in France"—a brake
For a bicycle, which is so
Revolutionary and
Efficient, I ask him if he
Can have it copied for me
In a model shop. "I do not
Use a model shop. I make them
Myself, in my spare time in the
Garage." "What do you do in the
Garage?" "I wash cars." No one speaks.
At last Léontine says, "There is
No place for a man like him
In France. No one will invest
Any money. They want big
Profits from the old machinery,

Making the old junk. The money
They put in gold in boxes
In the banks in Buenos Aires."
I look at him. He is in rags.
His cheeks are like splotches
Of red ink. In a year or so
He will be dead. If he had gone
To America in his youth,
Today he would be on the
Cover of *Time* magazine. But
He would never have written the
Poem about the midinette
And the camel, or the song
About the nuns who got drunk.
If only poverty was not
Killing him. I write an address.
"You can mail those plans to Detroit.
I am sure they would give you
A job. But like M'sieu le berger,
You would not like America."
When we leave the card is crumpled
On the floor. It is the law
Of the falling rate of profit.
I ask Léontine where she got
Her name. "Ah, but Kennet", you are
A poet and philosopher—
It was the name of the great
Courtesan, the mistress of
The philosophe Epicure."
At first I am too tipsy to
Appreciate this statement.
Then the full force of it hits me.
Here I am, living Landor's
Best piece of prose, more beautiful
Than anything in English
Outside of Gibbon, but not
In just the way he wrote it.
It is getting late. Signor
Picelli invites us to his house

For minestrone. He explains
His name. "Picelli—almost like the
Pope. I almost became Pope,
But alas, everyone knew my wife."
He stands in his loft, erect
In his slumping body, surrounded by
Dead white replicas of all
The sculpture of the ages,
And talks about aesthetics,
In English, French, and Italian.
Then he takes me aside and asks
If Marthe is broadminded.
I assure him she is and he
Shows us a series of little
Erotic sculptures, lovers in
All sorts of tangled embraces.
"All I can do now. My hand
Is gone. Dépourvu d'esprit—
Les plaisirs de mon vieux sang—
Et par la paresse." I am too
Stupid and polite to buy one.
"Mon vieux sang," Vitalis' words
The night he froze to death, over
Which I shuddered as a child.
As we are singing over the
Minestrone, he has a fit,
And the party breaks up.
We come out, back of the Gare
Montparnasse into the narrow
Alley, like a stage set in the
Dense November fog. Its name
Is the Passage du Départ.

A community of love is
A community of mutual
Indwelling, in which each member
Realizes his total
Liability for the whole.
A collectivity is like

A cancer disorganizing the
Organism which produced it.
The healthy organism
Itself, responds instantly,
As a whole, to the injury
To the slightest of its parts.
Those who by function, or the chance
Of historical accident,
Have mercifully been shut off
From the ravages of social
Paranoia and cancer
Still possess the remnants of
Community, and can begin
To widen and extend it.
This class, unfortunately,
Includes few white Americans.
Where it survives, community
Can transcend history only
By becoming self conscious,
And its first step must be the
Stopping of the insanity
Of commodity production,
And the substitution of free
Satisfaction of human needs.

Bienheureux sont les débonnaires
Car ils hériteront la terre.

O Paris, ses faubourgs anonymes!
O Paris, ses avenues disparues!
Paris, où la pauvreté était toujours la vertu.
Paris, où la Révolution vint et attend.
Paris, que vous n'auriez pas trouvé autour de la rue Scribe.
Le soleil qui s'couche dans les ruelles bornées derrière
      Clignancourt.
Belleville, la brume d'hiver, les lumières faibles.
Place République ténébreuse, les filles perdues se répandent
      invisiblement.
Rue de la Chapelle dans la bagarre de minuit.
Midi d'été, l'Avenue de l'Ouest bouillant avec les pauvres;

242

Ici on achète le boudin, le cheval, les fruits sales, les pièces
　　des vélos.
Les andouillettes de la rue des Rosiers, où je retrouve mon
　　Yiddish.
Avenue du Maine, "Bikini," le Dancing Nègre, le rhum
　　punch.
Saint Germain de Charonne garde un aspect villageois au
　　milieu de son petit cimetière en terrasse où repose
　　Magloire Bègue, secrétaire de Robespierre et amateur
　　de roses.
Le lion en pantoufles défend les souterrains à Denfert-
　　Rochereau.
Villette, la nuit étoilée, vide comme le Nevada.
Stalingrad, les escargots, la bière, le billard.
Vercingétorix, le poiré et le tric-trac.
Rue Daguerre, le calvados et les échecs.
Saint Denis, les oursins et la Saintonge avec
Un vieillard qui avait connu Louise Michel.
Rue Vieille-du-Temple, Gazelle chantant "Le Pont
　　Mirabeau,"
Son dos une cicatrice solide, grâce aux camps
　　de concentration.
Paris, de l'Internationale du sang et du chair.

Milosz' "Symphonie de Novembre":
"It will be exactly like this life. The same room.
Yes, my child, the same. At dawn the bird of time in the
　　foliage,
Pale as a corpse. Then the servants will get up,
And you will hear the frozen noises, in the hollow basins

"Of the fountains. O terrible, terrible youth! O empty heart!
It will be exactly like this life. There will be
The poor voices, the voices of Winter in old slums,
The glass mender singing his own duet,

"The broken grandmother under a dirty bonnet
Crying out the names of fish, the man with the blue apron,
Who spits into a hand worn by the wheelbarrow,
And yells nobody knows what, like the Angel of Judgment."

Lamarck's four laws. Carnot's three laws.
The organic composition
Of capital. The law of
The falling rate of profit.

Organization at the
Point of production.
Abolition of the wage system.

Once they made war with swords,
Now they make it by withholding,
Now here, now there, bread which a good
Father would deny to no one.

Under the somber Autumn sky
We walk in the deserted
Jardin des Plantes. All the plants
Wear straw pelisses for Winter.
Evening comes on, smoky
And blue, and then cold fine rain.
A sign:

                AVIS
            LES JEUX
                SONT
            INTERDITS
            DANS LE
            LABYRINTHE

The maigre November rain
Is falling on the Boulevard
Montparnasse. The streets are dark
Blue and dim. Tiny weak lights
Of bicycles wobble past,
Of men going to work before
Daylight. Garbage collectors
Bang cans, vegetable men
Make deliveries in a
Few open shops. The neon
Bar ornament glows through the

Steaming windows of the Dôme.
No breakfast, they are just cleaning up.
The beautiful monument
By the Closerie des Lilas
On the Avenue Observatoire
Is barely visible,
Glistening in the cold first dawn.
Morning comes up Port Royal,
Wet, and biting to the bone.
This is our last sight of the
Crowded little shops of Paris,
Tall houses leaning back from the
Narrow streets and the cold grey
Façades of the Boulevards,
And then the river, silken
In the rain, the coal and gravel
Barges whispering through the rain.
Gare d'Austerlitz exactly
Like all Monet's portraits of it.

It clears before noon. Let Autumn
Golden on the golden Loire,
On the land, rich and beautiful,
Like Italy, like America.

Most men present themselves as parts
Of some malignant collection,
And, as such, are evidently
Bent on their own extinction.
Only a tiny handful
Appear as conscious members of
A community, as persons.
Therefore, either men are
Incapable of love and damned,
Or most men are illusions.
But the term "most men" refers
To nothing more real than any
Contingent aspect of the world.
The quantified collection
Is unreal. There are no most men,

As there are no most trees or stars.
Behind the collection stands,
One by one, a person. And
Unless I can touch that person,
I am only making a mistake
In grades of illusion, as one
Who thinks the shadow of a rope
Is a snake. When I offer love
And receive injury or hate,
I have not dealt with a person,
But with a projection of myself.

The associations of
Paris confuse the issue.
Here where Tourney had a free hand
In his home town, royal
Boulevard architecture
Stands revealed in all its sterile
Provincial grandeur. Even
The age of Boucher could not
Equal one Roman piazza
Let alone Florence or Venice.
Louis Quinze architects were
Best at boudoirs.

There are two Bordeaux, one a
Port for the North Atlantic,
The other for Spain and Africa.
So the best people in town
Were the black feline Negroes
Working the docks or studying
At the university,
And the Sephardic Jews. The
Negroes are still there. The Jews—
Beyond the tomb of Montaigne,
At the end of a narrow
Street, is one of the best
Examples of Louis Quinze
Architecture. From a distance
The gable looks odd, crowned with

Two little bumps; nearer they
Become the curved tops of the
Tablets of the Law. In the
Forecourt is another tablet.
Five hundred names are arranged by
Families: Moses Cohen,
Rebecca Cohen, Samuel
Cohen, Sarah Cohen, Saul
Texeira, Ruth Texeira,
Leah Texeira, David Texeira—
The Nazis locked the entire
Jewish population in this
Small building, kept them without
Food and water for a few days,
Machine gunned them through the windows.
When they heard of such things, the
Pogrom loving Poles and the
Ukrainians revolted,
The Italians fought like tigers,
The French and Negro workers
Made Bordeaux industrially
Worthless to the Nazis. But
The citoyens did nothing.
Ribbentrop was once a wine
Salesman. Business was better
Than usual.

Bordeaux with its
Pencil stub towers—a bit of
France that is forever England.
The center of Protestantism,
The bailiwick of the country
Gentlemen and merchants who
Died such pathetic deaths, struggling
To introduce the ghost of
William of Orange, that morose,
Homosexual, progressive
Millionaire, to the France of
Marat, Hébert, Jacques Roux.
The poules become tarts, the arcade

Where they hustle looks like Soho,
And their faces are bitter
With guilt. The churches are neuter
Gothic and sadly jumbled,
But it must be admitted
The detached towers are an
Unforgettable sensation.
Sainte-Croix, our last sight of the
Beautiful Langue d'Oc Romanesque,
Like all of them, lovingly
Rebuilt by Abadie.
We load up on Château Ausone
And our little French freighter
Crawls moaning through the fog down the
Gironde, and out into the
Invisible Atlantic.
Behind us in the Bordeaux
Museum, Delacroix' "Greece Dying
At Missolonghi," ivory
And gold, burning and charred, the
Perfect farewell of France, the
Symbol of how many
Revolutions betrayed.

Midnight, the swollen half moon,
Setting in the warm seas, the wake
Seething with stars and nebulae
Of living phosphorescence.

"What is evil?" said Pilate.
This is the blood of Rahab,
Lifted upon high on the
Riven wood of the tree of
Paradise for the confounding
Of all nations.

Boehme's flagrat, the cross on
Which being turns to meaning,
And water turns back to wine.

Love who moves the sun and the other stars.

V

New York a grey haze with flights of
Pigeons wheeling above Harlem
As the boys on the rooftops
Whirl long poles and call them home.
The skyscrapers vanish quickly
Away and away forever.
As the observation car
Crosses the Harlem River
Past the tall red brick Berlinese-
Looking Negro housing projects,
The lights turn red, closing the way.
The Hudson sinks deeper and
Deeper into the blue until
Nothing is left but the black
Outline of the Catskills, the lights
Of the other shore, the soaring
Bridge over the long water
Wan in the end of evening.

Through direct knowledge of the
Dual, indirect knowledge of
All the others, the manifold
Of all the possible, passes
Toward the critical point where
It vanishes to reappear
As a growing kernel of
Direct knowledge of the others.

Toledo late in the night,
The factories roaring. Elkhart
Before dawn, a few street signs
Still blazing, the lights of lonely
Cars waiting at the crossings.
Gary, the red fires and purple
Fires of the mills in the red
And purple Winter sunrise.

Being alternates with non-being.
For millions of years Shiva sleeps,

For millions of years he dances.
The world flows from the void, the void
Drinks up the world. We assume
That this is a period
Of being, action, creation,
A time of Shiva's dancing.

My favorite painting in Chicago,
A little Cazin—October day,
A rising field, withered grass,
A dull sky, a pink roof, coral
And silver, grey green and ashes
Of roses. And Corot's Roman
Paintings. Society is
Immoral and immortal.
The fragments that survive can
Always laugh at the dead. But
A young man has only one
Chance and brief time to seize it.
Shang bronzes. What endures, what
Perishes. In the vacant
Lots where we built trenches after
One war, now there are foxholes.

The evidence for full direct
Knowledge, not of the dual,
But of the manifold other,
Under conditions known to us,
Is slight and sporadic and
Difficult to class as knowledge.
However, this may be due to
Its unanalyzable
Character in terms of a
Pattern of experience
Which for discursive knowledge
Of the world of consequence
We have made mechanically
Analytic. Certainly some
Knowledge of the other is
The universal content of

All mystical experience
And of much that is not so called.

We walk in the silver and grey
Afternoon along the Midway
And visit the neighborhood
Where I grew up and pass my old
Grammar school, now all Negro
Children. On the frosty air
From the northwest comes faintly
The odor of the stockyards,
Decadent now, and hardly
Perceptible, not the old-
Time rich stench. We walk back through
Washington Park in the windy
Early night, lights among the
Bare trees, the air thick with frost.
Dinner in one of the last
Good restaurants in America—
The Red Star Inn, the menu,
As the cooking, unchanged as
The highchair I used to sit in,
Still there in its corner.
The blissful Buddha face of
Sweets Williams driving the piano
Like a locomotive over
The stumblebum squalor of
The cheapest North Clark Street bar.
The entranced sadistic face
Of one girl who does the
Most cunnilingual strip in
The business, the customers
Like yawning hippopotami,
Not a dry fly in the house.
No other city deserves
North Clark Street, the B girls and
Dice girls in glen plaid suits and
Tailored blouses, the only
Sign of vice the fetishistic
Castled hair like Fuseli's tarts,

Spike heels and black net stockings.
"You look lonely, I am lonely too.
Would you enjoy a drink with me?"
The management prefers girls
With a college education.
The dice girl has a new boyfriend
From Hell's Kitchen who regales
Her with stories of the wonders
Of New York, and how tough he is.
At 3 a.m. he says, 'Hey,
Tomato, what do you say
To coppin' a mo'?" She says,
"Yes, darling, I am awfully tired,
I think it would be nice to leave."
Tonight she has taken any
Number of customers and
Primed and fingered three suckers
And sent them to meet her in
The dark hallway of her supposed
Apartment, where they met a
Sock full of sand. The B girls
Never bother with tea, but
Quickly toss off "triple gins,"
Three dollars worth of water.

V.I.T.R.I.O.L.
Visita interiora terrae
Rectificando invenies
Occultem lapidem. Seek
In the interior of
The earth, rectify, and you
Will discover the hidden stone.

In K.C. everyone, even
The whores and an appreciable
Number of Negroes, looks like
Truman. I go out with a
Black, deep bosomed, aquiline nosed
Girl like a Sudanese—no
Public place possible in

Kansas City, so we go
To the house of a friend, who
Turns out to be my train porter,
Drink beer and dance to records.
A city uninhabited
Except for a few Negroes
And some good Chinese paintings.

Calvinist and Liberal
Both strive to reduce moral
Action to the range of the
Objectively guaranteed.
The essential character
Of the moral act is its lack
Of objective guarantee.

In Kansas even the horses
Look like Landon, ugly parched
Faces like religious turtles,
The original'scissorbills.

Augustine, Luther, Kierkegaard,
The pragmatic leap in the dark.
Act loses reality,
Reality is equated
With mechanical stability,
Masochistic decision
Becomes hallucination,
A blind plunge out of being,
Sacrifice its own value—
The Nibelungen Spirit.

West from Newton a dust storm,
The air whirling and smothering,
All the bare trees painted with
Pale grey dust, a flock of crows
Crying through the dust, over
The stubble and young fall wheat
Grey with dust, the edge of the flock
Invisible in the dust.

The decline and fall of the
Capitalist system, born
In blood in the Thirty Years War.

A ruined country and a
Ruining people, the world
Would be better if Kansas
Were not in it. Dodge City,
Nearing the West, the air has changed,
Migrating ducks fly across
The full moon, a warm wind
Before a storm blows down the
Long continental slope from
The Rockies. Before Trinidad
It starts to snow, the high plains
Stretch away to the first mountains,
A thin wash of white under
The obscure moon, the air full of
Wandering snowflakes, saturated
With moonlight. Out at 3 a.m.,
Raton, a full blast of blizzard,
Impossible to stand up,
I sleep on a station bench.

"Early in the morning of
The next day, looking along
The horizon before us,
We saw that at one point it
Was faintly marked with pale
Indentations like the teeth
Of a saw. The distant lodges
Of the Arapahoes rising
Between us and the sky caused
This singular appearance."
Parkman, a boy on the
Oregon Trail, before he was
Terrified by the libidos
Of the Indians and turned to
His fourteen-volume epic

Of the triumph of anal
Over oral sexuality.

South of Raton by a small bus
To Taos, the dry grass with
Snow blowing through it looks like
Opossum fur. As the clouds
Scatter and the just-risen sun
Breaks out and lights up the mountains,
The landscape turns blue and silver
And pale wintry gold, with tatters
Of clouds hurrying to the
Edges of the sky. I am
Back home. This is my country.
All that back there is illusion.
The sign says Taos 86,
Cimarron 26, and all
The sick and liberated
Writresses and fairies vanish
Into the great abysm
Of pain and commodities
That is civilization.
The mountains come nearer and nearer,
Two punchers get on I knew once
On a ranch in Montana.
The bus radio plays cowboy
Songs, I read a novel by
Ernest Haycox, so much better than
The continued story about
The Jewish boy who doesn't
Want to get a job, and the
Serial about Henry James,
And the serial about Kafka
In each issue of the leading
Reviews. The moon just past full
Is setting in the cold western
Sky of early morning over
The headwaters of the Cimarron,
Over hills brushed with snow and

Junipers storm-encrusted
With new snow. The bus driver
Stops and waits. Everybody
Discusses some deer tracks on the
Road. Finally we go back
And dig out a car we were
Leading out of Eagle Nest.

Comet tails and sunspots suffice
To account for all history.

Taos mostly gone, pavements, neon,
Four times as many houses.
The natives, at least the Spanish,
Still friendly and hospitable.
Most of the people newcomers,
New Yorkers and Chicagoans,
Everyone a shady customer
Of some kind, spreading an air
Of fake over the whole town.
The Lawrence set like the surly
Aging employees of a mausoleum,
All still hating each other.
Frieda gone for the Winter
The Indian girls on the street
Still look as hot as ever.
Andrew Dasburg, one of the
Old masters of modern art,
Comes to my lecture and we
Talk of fine nights of drunken
Argument twenty years gone.
Black night, bright moon, Orion
Vast over Lawrence's ashes.

The white race approaches the end of
Its tether, withers on its frontiers.
Vulvas of flame open in the sun.
The glaciers grow, the cyclones move south,
A black Thales falls into a well.

The morning brilliant, the fields
Blazing with snow, a pile of
Perfumed fresh lumber, a shaggy
Black horse breathing steam into the
Glare.

It is likely that even
The most etherialized
Vision of the mystic is
Knowledge much as an amoeba
Might be said to know a man.

Back to Raton and north, past the
Long Sangre de Cristo chain
Running off to the southwest.
Night shuts over the Rockies,
Gloomy and thick. Over Kansas
Furious blizzards are raging.
Next day traffic is all bound up.
I go back to Pueblo and cross
By the Royal Gorge on the
Only train through. Skurries of
Snow under heavy sky, the
Mountain somber to the west,
The continent falling away
On my left. Suddenly the sun
Breaks out and shines through driving snow.
Two long-tailed magpies, black and white,
Fly past, dipping through the storm.

Up from the Industrial Age,
Forward to the Atomic Age,
Man moves from the clinamen
Of Newton's apple, towards
The catastrophe of the Kant-
Laplace hypothesis. Descartes'
Angels fall from their bicycles.

Royal Gorge, across the stream
On the red cliff face runs a flume

Which has leaked and festooned itself
And the grass and rocks with twelve-foot
Icicles. In the daycoach
Eleven baby hillbillies,
California bound, all crying
At once. Steam from the curving train,
Clouds, snow, snow-covered mountains,
Emerge and merge. At the summit
The sky clears as the sun sets
And the peaks stand out as huge
As Kanchanjunga in the
Early twilight—a plain two
To three miles across and ten
Miles long, then the forested
Lower slopes, then three thousand
Feet of snow-covered massif—
In the plain, bunch grass sticking
Out of the snow, and shaggy
Horses walking delicately
In the wind, cutting the snow crust
With sharp steps like deer. Smoke, snow,
And the winding headlight. I stand
On the platform in the storm,
At my feet west-running water.
At Grand Junction a great
Monadnock with a narrow
Streamer of cloud across it
Near the top. The moon at the
Tail of the train, through orchards,
Past the lights of houses
In the zero night. I worked here
Once, it was all range country then.
Provo, first dawn, thick snow on
The ground, low clouds, the obscure moon
High in the sky, neat compact
Mormon houses, the breakfast
Lights coming up in them. Lombardy
Poplars bare in the white fields.
The lives of men beginning
Again, remote in the dawn.

Complete direct knowledge of
The others as the self, of
All the others, of all selves
As self knowledge, would cause the
Knower to vanish from our world.
Of course the disciples of
The founders of religions
Make exactly this claim for
Their masters, Christ's Ascension
And Buddha's Paranirvana.

Salt Lake City, the Lion
On the Lion House watches
Thick flakes of wet snow falling
Between the old locust trees.
The people on the calm streets
Look healthy and happy. Here
America reached its finest
Expression, in the most peaceful
City in the country, maybe
Now in the world. The strong power
Of communion still blesses it,
Brigham Young's peace, carved with a sword.
The clear water running in
The gutters, the white and cream
Brick houses with green shutters,
The home-going crowds and the snow
Falling through windless air in
The wide streets, at the heart
Of all this are calm bygone
Men with eighteen wives.

Since in the act of love the
Others are known in the other
As loved by him, jealousy
Destroys the meaning of the
Love relationship, corrodes it,
At last makes it impossible.
This means literal destruction
Of being and is the only

Real Hell. Jealousy objects
To love because it arises
From its opposite, hate, the
Desire to exploit the other
For purposes of ignorance
And grasping. Of course, as in most
Things, what this civilization
Calls love is its opposite.
Its love is an endless struggle
For flashy commodities, rare
Frigid fucking for frigidaires.

Night across Utah, to the south-
West snowy pyramids speckled
With junipers going by like
White mammoths as I fall asleep.
At noon the next day rolling
Down the long grade through Joshua
Trees I see a highway sign
And realize I am in California.
The mountains ahead of me
Are the tail end of the
Panamints, beyond them the high
Arid White Mountains, the desert
Valley, and the Sierra
Nevadas with their long trails
Through illusion and vision.

The good and evil of the world
Are the reflections of the will
Of the owner of that world.
Contemplation can multiply
Illusion until consequence
Is utterly exhausted.
All matter is redeemed by man,
Hence in poisonous medicines
It is the sick themselves who are
The doctors and heal the poisons.

I come back to the cottage in
Santa Monica Canyon where

Andrée and I were poor and
Happy together. Sometimes we
Were hungry and stole vegetables
From the neighbors' gardens.
Sometimes we went out and gathered
Cigarette butts by flashlight.
But we went swimming every day,
All year round. We had a dog
Called Proclus, a vast yellow
Mongrel, and a white cat named
Cyprian. We had our first
Joint art show, and they began
To publish my poems in Paris.
We worked under the low umbrella
Of the acacia in the dooryard.
Now I get out of the car
And stand before the house in the dusk.
The acacia blossoms powder the walk
With little pills of gold wool.
The odor is drowsy and thick
In the early evening.
The tree has grown twice as high
As the roof. Inside, an old man
And woman sit in the lamplight.
I go back and drive away
To Malibu Beach and sit
With a grey-haired childhood friend and
Watch the full moon rise over the
Long rollers wrinkling the dark bay.

"It is those who are married
Who should live the contemplative
Life together. In the world
There is the long day of
Destruction to go by. But
Let those who are single, man
Torn from woman, woman from
Man, men altogether, women
Altogether, separate
Deathly fragments, each returning
And adhering to its own kind,

The body of life torn in two,
Let these finish the day of
Destruction, and those who have
United go into the
Wilderness to know a new
Heaven and a new earth."

There are those who spend all their lives
Whirling in the love and hate
Of the deities they create.

Contemplation is direct
Knowledge, beyond consequence,
Ignorance, appetite, grasping
Of possibility. The
Contemplative knows himself
As the focus of the others,
And he knows the other, the
Dual, as the mirror of
Himself and all the others,
The others as the mirror
Of himself and the dual.

Christmas Eve, unseasonably cold,
I walk in Golden Gate Park.
The Winter twilight thickens.
The park grows dusky before
The usual hour. The sky
Sinks close to the shadowy
Trees, and sky and trees mingle
In receding planes of vagueness.
The wet pebbles on the path
Wear little frills of ice like
Minute, transparent fungus.
Suddenly the air is full
Of snowflakes—cold, white, downy
Feathers that do not seem to
Come from the sky but crystallize
Out of the air. The snow is
Unendurably beautiful,

Falling in the breathless lake,
Floating in the yellow rushes.
I cannot feel the motion
Of the air, but it makes a sound
In the rushes, and the snow
Falling through their weaving blades
Makes another sound. I stand still,
Breathing as gently as I can,
And listen to these two sounds,
And watch the web of frail wavering
Motion until it is almost night.
I walk back along the lake path
Pure white with the new snow. Far out
Into the dusk the unmoving
Water is drinking the snow.
Out of the thicket of Winter
Cattails, almost at my feet,
Thundering and stamping his wings,
A huge white swan plunges away.
He breaks out of the tangle,
And floats suspended on gloom.
Only his invisible
Black feet move in the cold water.
He floats away into the dark,
Until he is a white blur
Like a face lost in the night,
And then he is gone. All the world
Is quiet and motionless
Except for the fall and whisper
Of snow. There is nothing but night,
And the snow and the odor
Of the frosty water.

The contemplative begins
By putting aside as far
As he can all appetite,
All wish to reap consequence
From possibility, and then
Cultivates disinterested
Knowledge of himself and of

The simplest things, knowing them
As really perspectives into
The others. By this means he
Rises to the first direct
Acquaintance with another,
With the dual as a person,
And more and more perfectly
Knowing the dual, rises
Towards the direct knowledge of
All the others, the infinite,
Absolute society.

The beginning of truth is
Wonder. He who wonders shall
Reign and he who reigns shall rest.

Seven days now, in the midst
Of the rainy season, the
Weather has been dry and bright,
In the evening the air
Is hazy with exhalations
Of the drying forest. Night
And morning the dewfall
Is tremendous; and there is
Frost on the bottoms and in
The open glades. New Year's night,
I walk in the moonlight. In the
Immaculate night the moonbeams
Are like needles. Great bars of
Moonhaze buttress the redwoods.
As I cross the meadow little
Pannicles of ice on the grass
Tinkle against my shoes.
There is a glory around
The head of my shadow, a soft,
Phosphorescent, lunar rainbow.
Over the vast downs, between
The redwoods and the sea, a few
Cattle and sheep move slowly
Or not at all. Then nothing moves.

No light is visible nearer
Than the moon and the stars. Far off,
The world falls like a bomb towards
Its own destruction. I have
Ceased to hear it. I no longer
Have any theories about it.
I no longer have any
Philosophy. All of my
Capacity for tragedy
Is exhausted. I tread softly,
Listening to the earth in the
Moonlight. Peace flows without stopping.
The peace is illimitable
The clear glory is without end.

The contemplative heart, and
Reciprocally the other,
Rise above the levels of
Consequence, appetite, and
Discursive knowledge, with their
Limitations of time and space,
Coming to be and passing away,
And come to know each other
More and more directly. The
Fullness of being is the
Direct knowledge of all the
Others with its love and joy.

When abandoned by Zeus, the
Body of Leda's swan was
Murdered by jealous Electra.

Under the second moon the
Salmon come, up Tomales
Bay, up Papermill Creek, up
The narrow gorge to their spawning
Beds in Devil's Gulch. Although
I expect them, I walk by the
Stream and hear them splashing and
Discover them each year with

A start. When they are frightened
They charge the shallows, their immense
Red and blue bodies thrashing
Out of the water over
The cobbles; undisturbed, they
Lie in the pools. The struggling
Males poise and dart and recoil.
The females lie quiet, pulsing
With birth. Soon all of them will
Be dead, their handsome bodies
Ragged and putrid, half the flesh
Battered away by their great
Lust. I sit for a long time
In the chilly sunlight by
The pool below my cabin
And think of my own life—so much
Wasted, so much lost, all the
Pain, all the deaths and dead ends,
So very little gained after
It all. Late in the night I
Come down for a drink. I hear
Them rushing at one another
In the dark. The surface of
The pool rocks. The half moon throbs
On the broken water. I
Touch the water. It is black,
Frosty. Frail blades of ice form
On the edges. In the cold
Night the stream flows away, out
Of the mountain, towards the bay,
Bound on its long recurrent
Cycle from the sky to the sea

The road which can be travelled is
Not the right road. The word which can
Be spoken is not the true word.

Most often God has been the name
Given to the most powerfully
Known person behind all the

Perspectives into all the
Others. Each contemplative
Has, usually, his own god
Whom he has come to know because
That person, however remote,
Has responded directly
To him. Theoretically
All the universe could be
The conversation of one
Person, the god of mystical
Monotheism. (The Sufi,
For instance, not of course
The orthodox Christian, who
Is not a monotheist.)
It seems, from the testimony
Of all religious experience,
That there are as many gods
As there are persons. When the
Object of contemplation
Is a person whom we know
Also as another like
Ourselves in the universe of
Possibility and consequence,
We do not customarily
Think of that person as a
God. But this is merely a
Convention of terminology.

Li Po and I both like to
Look at waterfalls. Deep in
The mountains, I turn my skis
And pause where black and white water
Breaks through the snow. All about
My feet are loose crystals of ice
Formed by the mist, as big as hands.
After a long time I turn
And drop into the valley,
Maneuvering swiftly over
Tumbled avalanche cones and snow
Covered rocks and through sparse thickets

Of dwarf maples, their trunks not
Much thicker than my thumb and pale
Silver grey. Their winged samaras
Still cling to them, a paler,
Silver yellow. Each twig
Is tipped with buds, deep crimson,
Overlaid with fine black lines
Like drops of congealing blood.
Here and there on the snow is
A skeleton of a leaf, thin
And frail as an x-ray picture,
Its flesh eaten by Winter.

Striving to perpetuate
Itself endlessly, illusion
Endures only an instant;
In the face of contemplation
It vanishes in not-being.
Appetite, the struggle of
Form and formlessness; desire,
The reversal of the waste
Of the historic process.

Love is the subjective
Aspect of contemplation.
Sexual love is one of
The most perfect forms of
Contemplation, as far as it
Is without ignorance, grasping,
And appetite. As far as it
Attempts to use the dual to
Manipulate the changing
Relations of consequence
And possibility, it
Is not love but hate.

There are hardly any blossoms
Left on the apple and pear trees
In the broken orchard where I
Have walked so many Springs.

I did not see them this year, white
And splendid under the full moon.
Now in the evening as the fog
Comes in across the new moon,
I bury my face in one last
Cluster of blossom and remember
The mockingbirds in the South,
That sang all through the brilliant
Night, as we lay arm in arm.

Knowledge of the others through
The dual is probably not
The only method of knowing
In the sense that all men must
Have a monogamous lover
Or a monotheistic god.
Some persons seem to be linked
Like atoms of oxygen,
Others not. But the nature
Of reality would seem to
Demand that in each specific
Act of love there be one other.
Duality is a condition
Of direct knowledge. However,
The dual can be found in the
Void of the one or in the
Fullness of all the others,
Just as they are found in it.

The afternoon ends with red
Patches of light on the leaves
On the northeast canyon wall.
My tame owl sits serenely
On his dead branch. A foolish
Jay squalls and plunges at him.
He is ignored. The owl yawns
And stretches his wings. The jay
Flies away screaming with fright.
My king snake lies in inert
Curves over books and papers.

Even his tongue is still, but
His yellow eyes are judicial.
The mice move delicately
In the walls. Beyond the hills
The moon is up, and the sky
Turns to crystal before it.
The canyon blurs in half light.
An invisible palace
Of glass, full of transparent
People, settles around me.
Over the dim waterfall
The intense promise of light
Grows above the canyon's cleft.
A nude girl enters my hut,
With white feet, and swaying hips,
And fragrant sex.

               Although they might
In theory all emanate
From the contemplative himself,
We assume the others as real.
In a sense all persons are
Emanations of each other.
Reality is like a
Magnetic field with an infinite
Number of poles. We can know
At least the dual directly
And the others through the dual.
This is a fact of experience.
Like all experience, it is
Not subject to proof since proof
Is discursive description
Of consequence. In the dual
Each appears to the other
As his power, as the sum
Total of all the possible.

The reason why the illusion
Of consequence can exert
Its influence is to be found

In the laws of the rhythm
Of being; action is always
Followed by rest, as the labor
Of the day by sleep. As the
Contemplative drowses, the
Five daughters of illusion
Appear. The world of limited
Experience is the dream
Of being. We think of this
As the time of Shiva's dancing.
It is not. What we call being
Is illusion, the dream of Shiva.
It is an instant or a million
Times a million years before he wakes.

Two years since I have been in
The Fillmore District. I go down
And walk around aimlessly.
As I pass the house where ——
Used to work, she appears at the
Window, very excited.
I go in, she kisses me
And seems delighted to see me.
She says, "I'll knock off for an hour
And we'll go get a drink."
As a matter of fact we go
To lunch. I tell her I have
Been away, and she says, "Oh,
So have I—so we didn't
Miss each other. Where've you been?
I thought of you a lot."
"Europe." "Gee, swell, you must
Tell me all about it. I have
Been having a baby." "That's fine.
I didn't know you had an
Old man." "I don't." "Who's the father?"
"I don't know, some customer.
But he's a swell baby, I guess
I pulled the lever just right and
Hit the jackpot. Anyway,

He's white. I wanted to nurse him,
So I turned square for a while."
She is all excited and
Elated, laughing, eyes glistening,
Full of happiness about
Her baby. "What do you do
With him while you're working?"
"My mother takes care of him,
You see, I've got another one,
A three year old boy, he's a
Regular Dempsey." (——
Is about twenty-five, the
Legend still lives.) "You ought to see
Him." "I'd like to." "Would you honest?"
"Sure." "Honest? Look, how about
Coming to dinner tomorrow.
I'd like you to meet my mother,
Too." "Fine." "OK, I've got to
Get back to work now. Gee, you'll
Like the oldest guy. I got
Him out of the grab bag, too."

The leading philosopher
Of the University
Of California asks me,
"Why do you poets charge so much
Money?" "I beg your pardon.
What was that?" "Why do poets charge
So much? I would read poetry
If it wasn't so expensive.
The other day I was in
Sather Gate Bookshop and picked up
A book of poetry. You
Wouldn't believe it, but the price
Was two dollars and it contained
Less than a hundred pages!"
The logical positivist—
Life's answers are vended by
Slot machines. Just drop a nickel.
The magical Weltanschauung

Of the Australian bushman.
My lamp is small and bright
In the darkness of the night.

Said Pilate, "What is proof?" and washed
His hands before the multitude.

The age drives mad its saviors,
Courtesan and beggar turn
Bolshevik agitators.
Insanity is the crippling
Of the organ of reciprocity.

Off from the climbing road fall
Away folded shadows of
Mountains, range on moony range.
Under the waning moon the great
Valley like a hazy sea,
The town like the riding lights
Of fishing boats. The mountain
Peaks white and indistinct, their
Congruent tops merged in a high
Undulant horizon. Faint
Bells come up from the meadows.

The insecurity and
Ambiguity of modern
Culture is a reflection
Of the instability
Of the love relationship.
Art provides instruments of
Contemplation. Contemplation
Is the satisfaction of fulfilled
Love relationships, union with
The beloved object. If love is
Invalided, the whole fabric
Of the world culture crumbles.

Little Blue Lake—violet
Green swallows skimming above

Their reflections and dipping
To sip the water from their
Imaged beaks. Deep, deep and still,
Black and grey cliffs and white snow,
And the pale pure blue drowned ice.

Tara, the Power of Buddha;
Kali, the Power of Shiva;
Artemis, Apollo's sister;
The Wisdom of the Lord; the
Shekinah, Jehovah's Glory;
Mary the Mother of God;
Magdalene, the Bride of Christ;
Act and power, the twin lovers;
Each reflects the other like
The two chambers of the heart.

The lavabo of Pilate
Was the Graal of the Passover.

Once more we climb up the long
Gentle grade to Chagoopa
Plateau and look back, through the
Twisted foxtail pines growing
In the white talus, at the
Vast trough of Big Arroyo.
Again as always the Clark
Nutcrackers, grey, black and white,
Caw in the trees. Life repeats
Itself. We have camped here so
Many times by the shores of
Moraine Lake, the beautiful
Kaweah Peaks reflected
In the water, blue damsel
Flies on all the rushes.
In the evening, nighthawks
Will cry and dart through the air,
Dive, turn and swoop up again,
The twisting blades of their wings
Making a special growling roar

Like no other sound at all.
We will swim night and morning,
Catch golden trout in the creek,
See the water ouzel's nest
In the waterfall. Bear will
Bounce away from us as we
Wander between the open
Columns of the arid forest
Through the blue and white dwarf lupins.
In Sky Parlor Meadow there
Will be dozens of deer. The
Antlers of the bucks will look
Like dead branches above the
Tall rushes in the little lost
Marsh. The crimson bryanthus
And white Labrador tea will
Bloom by the lake as always.
In the evening crossing
The great meadow the sunset
On the water in the sedge
Will look like green and citron
Brocade, shot with copper and
Gold and blue—and the killdeer
Crying around us. And as
We come near camp, the nighthawks,
Those happy, happy birds,
Plunging over the lake again.
So the nighthawks cried over me
As I walked through smoky saffron
Twilights in the parks and long
Streets of Chicago in my
Entranced childhood. It is
Wise to keep the pattern of
Life clear and simple and filled
With beautiful and real things.
The round may be narrow enough.
The rounds of the world are narrower.

A truly radical, naïve,
Religious empiricism

Would describe all experience
In terms of its central fact.
The workings of the mind, the
Will, the physical and the
Transcendental worlds, would be seen
From the viewpoint of the
Contemplative immersed in
Contemplation. Reality
In a concourse of contemplatives.

Big Horn Plateau—four ravens,
Two hawks, one sandpiper, foxes
Barking in the rocks, the wool
Of wild sheep clinging to dead trees.
The voices of the thunder, all
The supernatural voices
Of the world, lightning striking
Continuously against the
Kaweahs, then the Kings-Kern peaks.
Here high above timberline,
Busy animalcules swim
In the cold volatile water.
In the frosty moonlight the
Burro is restless. Coyotes
Howl close to camp all night long.

At the center of every
Universe, which flows from him
And back to him again is a
Contemplator; there are millions
Of universes, each with its
Contemplator, in a grain of sand.
Every entity, real or
Imagined, dust mote or hero
Of fiction, is one face of a
Contemplative—reality,
Their infinite conversation.

At twelve thousand feet, the perfume
Of the phlox is like a drug.

276

Far off, the foxtail forest
On Big Horn Plateau is orange
And black-green stubble. Clouds are
Rising in the distance beyond
Milestone and Thunder Mountains.
I glissade down the long snow bank
Of penitentes to the shores
Of Tulainyo Lake, barren
As the moon. I break the thin
Crust of bubbly white ice and
Drink the black tasteless water.
I climb to the final ridge
And look out of the windows
In the fourteen thousand foot
Arête. At my feet are the
Bluest polemonium and
The most crimson primrose, and far
Away, the russet Inyo
Mountains rise through grey desert heat.
In the evening by the flaring
Campfire of timberline wood,
Full of pitch and incense, I read
Buddha's farewell to his harem
And watch the storm move in the night,
The lightning burning a fire
From peak to peak, far below me.

Christ—the good people are the
Bad people and the bad people
Are the good people. The world
Is going to be destroyed
Any minute now, so live.
And Buddha—at the center
Of being is the act of
Contemplation, unqualified,
Unique, unpredicable.

As long as we are lost
In the world of purpose
We are not free. I sit

In my ten foot square hut.
The birds sing. The bees hum.
The leaves sway. The water
Murmurs over the rocks.
The canyon shuts me in.
If I moved, Bashō's frog
Would splash in the pool.
All Summer long the gold
Laurel leaves fell through space.
Today I was aware
Of a maple leaf floating
On the pool. In the night
I stare into the fire.
Once I saw fire cities,
Towns, palaces, wars,
Heroic adventures,
In the campfires of youth.
Now I see only fire.
My breath moves quietly.
The stars move overhead.
In the clear darkness
Only a small red glow
Is left in the ashes.
On the table lies a cast
Snakeskin and an uncut stone.

There is no need to assume
The existence of a god
Behind the community
Of persons, the community
Is the absolute. There is no
Future life because there is
No future. Reality
Is not conditioned by time,
Space, ignorance, grasping.
The shift from possibility
To consequence gives rise to
The convention of time. At
The heart of being is the act of
Contemplation, it is timeless.

Since Isis and Osiris
Many gods and goddesses
Have ridden the boats of
The sun and the moon. I stand
On the hill above my hut
And watch the sun set in the
Fog bank over the distant
Ocean. Shortly afterward
The moon rises, transparent
In the twilight above the
Mountain. There is nobody
In them this evening. I
Am sure they are empty, that
I am alone in the great
Void, where they journey, empty
Through the darkness and the light.

Deep in myself arise the rays
Called Artemis and Apollo,
Helios, Luna, Sun and Moon,
Flowing forever out into
The void, towards the unknown others.

The heavens and hells of man,
The gods and demons, the ghosts of
Superstition, are crude attempts;
The systems of philosophers,
The visions of religion,
Are more or less successful
Mythological descriptions
Of knowing, acting, loving—
You are Shiva, but you dream.

It is the dark of the moon.
Late at night, the end of Summer,
The Autumn constellations
Glow in the arid heaven.
The air smells of cattle, hay,
And dust. In the old orchard
The pears are ripe. The trees

Have sprouted from old rootstocks
And the fruit is inedible.
As I pass them I hear something
Rustling and grunting and turn
My light into the branches.
Two raccoons with acrid pear
Juice and saliva drooling
From their mouths, stare back at me,
Their eyes deep sponges of light.
They know me and do not run
Away. Coming up the road
Through the black oak shadows, I
See ahead of me, glinting
Everywhere from the dusty
Gravel, tiny points of cold
Blue light, like the sparkle of
Iron snow. I suspect what it is,
And kneel to see. Under each
Pebble and oak leaf is a
Spider, her eyes shining at
Me with my reflected light
Across immeasurable distance.

THE HEART'S GARDEN
THE GARDEN'S HEART

Kyoto, 1967

For
Mary
Katharine
Carol

THE HEART'S GARDEN
THE GARDEN'S HEART

I

Young rice plants are just being
Transplanted. Tea bushes are
Low and compact. Eggplants are
Still under their little tents.
K'oto meadows, samisen
Lakes, mountain drums; water flutes
Falling all night in moonlight.
Migrating birds twitter on
The roofs. Azaleas bloom.
Summer opens. A man of
Sixty years, still wandering
Through wooded hills, gathering
Mushrooms, bracken fiddle necks,
And bamboo shoots, listening
Deep in his mind to music
Lost far off in space and time.
The valley's soul is deathless.
It is called the dark woman.
The dark woman is the gate
To the root of heaven and earth.
If you draw her out like floss
She is inexhaustible.
She is possessed without effort.
It was a green jacket, a green
Jacket with a yellow lining.
When will the heartbreak stop?
It was a green jacket, a green
Jacket with a yellow skirt.
When will the heartbreak go?
The evergreen pines grow more
Green as Spring draws to an end.
Yellow rice blades in blue water.

Pausing in my sixth decade
At the end of a journey
Around the earth—where am I?
I am sitting on a rock
Close beside a waterfall
Above Kurama Hot Springs
In the hills above Kyoto.
So I have sat by hundreds,
In the Adirondacks and
The Green Mountains of Vermont,
In the Massif Central, Alps,
Cascades, Rockies, Sierras,
Even Niagara long, long
Ago in a night of snow.
The water speaks the same language.
It should have told me something
All these years, all these places,
Always saying the same thing.
I should have learned more than I did,
My wit ought to have been more.
I am now older than I was,
In Winters and in lore.
What can I see before me
In the water's smoke and mist?
I should have learned something. "Who
Am I? What can I do? What can I
Hope?" Kant on Euler's bridges
Of dilemma in Koenigsberg.
Somewhere in some topology
The knots untie themselves,
The bridges are all connected.
Is that true? How do you know?
"What is love?" said jesting Pilate
And would not stay for an answer.
I have asked many idle
Questions since the day I could speak.
Now I have many Winters
But very few answers.

Age has me bestolen on
Ere I it wist.
Ne might I see before me
For smoke nor for mist. The smoke
And mist of the waterfall
Shifts and billows. The double
Rainbow remains constant.
There are more years behind me
Than years ahead, and have been
For a very long time. What
Remains in either pan of
The unstable balances of time?
Childbirth, love, and ecstasy
Activate nerves otherwise
Never used and so are hard
To recall, and visions are
The measure of the defect
Of vision. I loved. I saw.
All the way down to Kyoto,
And high above me on all
The ridges are temples full of
Buddhas. This village of stone
Carvers and woodcutters is
Its own illimitable Buddha world.
The illuminated live
Always in light and so do
Not know it is there as fishes
Do not know they live in water.
Under the giant cypresses
Amongst the mossy stones and
Bamboo grass there are white stars
Of dwarf iris everywhere.
The forest is filled with incense.
Boys' Day, the giant wind carp
Float in the breeze of early
Summer over all the houses
Of this mountain village.
The light, cheap, paper ones do.
The more durable cloth ones
Hardly lift and sway at all.

There are rocks on the earth
More durable than the
Constellations of heaven.
Gold leaves of feather bamboo
Fall through the warm wind of May
On to the white rectangle
Of raked gravel in the temple
Garden. Why does the bamboo shed
Its leaves at this time of year?
Smoky, oppressively hot,
The evening comes to an end.
An uguisu sings in the gnarled pine.
The cuckoos call in the ginko trees,
Just like they do in the old poems.
Swallows mate on the telephone wires.
A wood pigeon, speckled like
A quail, drinks from the dew basin.
The new leaves are just coming in.
The bamboos look like green gold smoke.
In the weavers' quarter
Beyond the temple walls,
As the noises of the day cease
I can hear the throb and clack
Of thousands of home looms.
Nishikigi—but no ghosts rise.
Gold fish swim in the moat, red
As fire, they burn in the brown
Water. The moat guards the scriptures
From fire, but the Buddha word
Is burning like the dry grass on
The Indian hills and like the stars.
How easy it is for men
To do right—the submarine
Green of young maple leaves on moss,
Fourteen trees and some earth bare
Of all but moss, and the light
Like Cours Mirabeau in Aix
Before greed destroyed it.
The turtle is the symbol
Of obscenity, but all

The moats that guard the scriptures
Are planted with honorable
Turtles. Turtle-san, protect
The Three Jewels, as the lewd
Pigeons in the air protect
The Great Void. When they rut and beg
In the gravel garden, they fill
Their craws with uncut stones.
"Vectors of reticulation."
We are defined by the webs
Of ten thousand lines of force.
Rocks surrounded by currents
Of raked gravel. Stripes of tigers
Playing in the bamboo shade.
Lichens on ruined dragon stones.
"When I see the wild chrysanthemum
Blooming in the crannies
Of the cliff, I try to forget
The glories of the capital."
The water ouzel walks on
The bottom under the torrent
And builds her nest behind the
Waterfall. Kurama River,
Kaweah River, it is
The same water ouzel although
It is a different species.

III

Gathering early morning
Mushrooms, the music of the
Waterfall washes my ears.
Jumbled rocks clog the clear stream
But the trout love the whirlpools
And riffles. K'ao P'an Tsai Kien.
Two thousand years ago that was
A synonym for happiness—
"Find a hut by a mountain stream."

Hard as stone, water glitters
Like a diamond, and makes a huge
Mountain towering into
The clouds, and carves out canyons
Ten thousand feet deep, and caps
The poles. The same water is
An invisible vapor
Which materializes
When it comes near the mountain.
Here, where bones and mud piled up
And turned to stone and made this
Mountain, the sea once stretched from
Horizon to horizon.
Deep under the shallow sea,
And in the monk's rosary
Amber remembers the pine.
Millions of pearls in the mist
Of the waterfall added
Together make a rainbow.
Deep in the heart one pearl glows
With ten million rainbows.
Weary of the twin seas of
Being and not-being, I
Long for the mountain of bliss
Untouched by the changing tides.
Deep in the mountain wilderness
Where nobody ever comes,
Only once in a while something
Like the sound of a far off voice,
The low rays of the sun slip
Through the dark forest and gleam
In pools on the shadowy moss.
Wild flowers and grass grow on
The ancient ceremonial
Stairs. The sun sinks between the
Forested mountains. The swallows
Who nested once in the painted
Eaves of the palaces of
The young prince are flying

This evening between the homes
Of woodcutters and quarrymen.
More ancient by far than the stairs
Are the cyclopean walls
Of immense, dry laid stones covered
With moss and ferns. If you approach
Quietly and imitate their
Voices, you can converse all day
With the tree frogs who live there.
Peach petals float on the stream
Past the rubbish of the village.
Twilight gathers in the mountain
Village. Peach petals scatter
On the stream at the boom of
The evening bell. All past and
Future sounds can be heard in
A temple bell. The mountain
Goes on being a mountain,
And the sea, a sea, but life
Is frail as a petal in
A world like an insect's shell.
I sit in the hot spring and
Wash my body, spotless from
Its creation, in radiant
Waters, virgin and electric
From the earth womb, pillowed on
Water, a pebble in my mouth.
Tired of the twin peaks of plus
And minus, I float in the
Unruffled sea.

IV

Water is always the same—
Obedient to the laws
That move the sun and the other
Stars. In Japan as in

California it falls
Through the steep mountain valleys
Towards the sea. Waterfalls drop
Long musical ribbons from
The high rocks where temples perch.
Ayu in the current poise
And shift between the stones
At the edge of the bubbles.
White dwarf iris heavy with
Perfume hang over the brink.
Cedars and cypresses climb
The hillsides. Something else climbs.
Something moves reciprocally
To the tumbling water.
It ascends the rapids,
The torrents, the waterfalls,
To the last high springs.
It disperses and climbs the rain.
You cannot see it or feel it.
But if you sit by the pool
Below the waterfall, full
Of calling voices all chanting
In a turmoil of peace,
It communicates itself.
It speaks in the molecules
Of your blood, in the pauses
Between your breathing. Water
Flows around and over all
Obstacles, always seeking
The lowest place. Equal and
Opposite, action and reaction,
An invisible light swarms
Upward without effort. But
Nothing can stop it. No one
Can see it. Over and around
Whatever stands in the way,
Blazing infinitesimals—
Up and out—a radiation
Into the empty darkness
Between the stars.

V

The water in a bottle
Has a bottle shape. A girl
In a dress has a girl shape.
The girl contains the dress.
The stone alone on the ground
Makes a sound like a sound.
The carp in the temple pool
Of the vegetarians
Grow forever. Where no waves
Wash the myriad sands
The thousand birds do not come.
Forty million school children
Sightseeing. Forty thousand
Old ladies praying. The prayer
Gong never stops ringing. Around
The corner past the formal
Garden, nobody climbs the
Mountain path to the waterfalls,
Where a ninety year old woman
Worships the Earth Womb,
Singing in a loud falsetto,
And clapping her hands,
As the waterspout splashes
On her thin white hair
And withered breasts.
After a long time walking
Up and down the long hall
And looking at the thousand
Kwannons through the incense smoke
And candle light I realize
That each one looks different.
The curve of the lips, the regard
Of the eye, is never quite
The same, never exactly the same
Gesture of the blessing hands.
He who hears the world's cry.
Thirty three thousand thirty three
Heads, each with a hundred arms

And eleven faces.
Unalike.
Chidori, chidori, crying
Kannon, Kannon, Kannon, Kannon.
Each sandpiper has a thousand
Wings. The birds of midocean
Leave the deep sea only to breed.
Japan is an island empire
With twenty million women
Each with ten thousand giggles
Every day. But consider
This heavy eyed art student
With hair to her knees
On the lawn of the museum.
She has just finished smoking
A marijuana cigarette.
Now she is being tickled
By her lover.
        As my horse's hooves
Splashed through the clear water
Of the ford at Sado the
Ten thousand birds rose crying
About us.
        Chidori, chidori,
Kannon, Kannon,
          Each bird with
Ten thousand wings.
           He who hears
The crying of all the worlds.
At the end of an avenue
Of boars, like a line of sphinxes,
Is the temple of Marichi,
Patroness of geisha and whores,
And goddess of the dawn. The girl
Beside me tells me she was
A great Indian prostitute
Who was really a incarnate
Bodhisattva. The girl herself
Turned out to be a Communist.
I will not enter Nirvana

Until all sentient creatures are saved.
There is a street fair around
The Shinto shrine across the street
And its booths have overwhelmed
The precincts of Marichi.
It is their annual children's festival.
In the long warm evening
The mountains unfold above
Kamo River like a fan
Of wet silk dipped in thin ink.
At Daisenji the abbot's
Garden consists of two cones
Of gravel heaped to the angle
Of repose, surrounded by
A herring bone sea of raked
Gravel. Between the cones
Devadatta has thrown an empty
Film box, red and yellow,
The colors of fire. We meet
And touch and pass on, as log
Meets log in midocean.
On the screen in the guest house
Is a fan with a cock quail
Crying out alone amongst
Snow bound reeds. Deep evening.
I walk home and see
The greatest of the gravel
Gardens of enlightenment,
A tire tracked gas station yard
With seven empty oil cans,
And a rack of used tires, and
A painting of an imbecile
Tiger in red and yellow fire.
The spread of the ripples
Is not due to its size
But is proportionate
To the hidden power
In the stone thrown in the pool.
The waves of the sea have
A number, the sands of the

Shores have a number, the birds
Of the air have a number.
There is no number for the
Saviors of the universes.

VI

The Eve of Ch'ing Ming—Clear Bright,
A quail's breast sky and smoky hills,
The great bronze gong booms in the
Russet sunset. Late tonight
It will rain. Tomorrow will
Be clear and cool once more. One more
Clear, bright day in this floating life.
The slopes of Mt. Hiei are veiled
In haze for the last day of Spring.
Spring mist turns to Summer haze
And hides the distant mountains,
But the first evening breeze
Brings the scent of their flowers.
I say a few words and the haze
Lifts from Mt. Hiei and trees
And temples and climbing people
Stand out as sharp as glass.
Three red pigeons on the sunbaked
Gravel, murmuring like the
Far off voices of people
I loved once. The turtles sleep
On the surface of the moat.
If belief and anxiety,
Covetousness and grasping,
Be banished from experience
Of any object whatever,
Only its essence remains,
Only its ultimate being.
He who lives without grasping
Lives always in experience
Of the immediate as the

Ultimate. The solution
Of the problem of knowing
And being is ethical.
Epistemology is moral.
The rutting cock pigeons fill
Their craws with cob from the wall.
Each has his territory,
Where, already this season,
He has dug a hole as big
As a tea cup. They defend
The holes against intrusion
Like they quarrel over the hens.
The knot tied without a rope
Cannot be untied. The seven
Bridges of Koenigsberg cannot
Be crossed but you can always
Go for a swim in the river.
The lower leaves of the trees
Tangle the sunset in dusk.
Awe perfumes the warm twilight.
St. John of the Cross said it,
The desire for vision is
The sin of gluttony.
The bush warbler sings in the
Ancient white pine by the temple
Of the Buddha of Healing.

VII

Tea drinking, garden viewing,
The voices of Japanese
Women are like happy birds.
A calico cat rolls in
The sun on the silky moss.
At the end of the branches
The youngest maple leaves are
As red as they will be again
This Autumn when they are old.

Another cat, brown as a mink.
Most Japanese don't like cats.
The monks at this temple are
Eccentrics. However in
The daytime their cats wear bells.
Birds are nesting in the maples.
The women are admiring
The iris and waterlilies.
Beyond the wall—Nishikigi—
The click of the looms—
In all this quarter they are
Weaving obis.
          "All day I
Work in the click of the looms.
At night I go out and play
Pachinko amidst the clinks
Of a hundred pinball machines."
The goddess of mercy has
A hundred arms. The steel balls
Fall from heaven to hell,
Bouncing through the wickets
Of circumstance. On the field
Of Law? On the field of chance.
Where Krishna drove, Arjuna fought.
All over Japan pinballs fall
Like the myriad gonads of the
Human race through history.
The clicks of the looms, the clinks
Of the wickets, are the random
Ticking of organic time.
Shizu, shizu, shizu, yo—
Bobbins whisper through the threads,
Endlessly repeating, "If
Only I could somehow make
Yesterday today."
Currite ducentes subtegmina currite fusi.
Two black swallow tailed butterflies
Hover over the two cats.
They are too old and wise to mind.
A cicada cries in the heat

296

Of late afternoon and then
A telephone bell answers him.
Is this right? Should Buddhist monks
Have telephones? Who hears
The worlds cry out in pain?
A young man with immense teeth
And stiff hair is working himself
Into a lather explaining
The contemplative mysteries
Of the garden to five
Remarkably beautiful
Young women. He sees neither
Garden nor girls. He sounds like
A cheerleader. A baby
Breaks away from its mother,
The lady who sells tickets,
And runs across the limitless sea
Of raked gravel, just where
The film box was yesterday.
Life is unruly in the
Zendo. What is the secret,
The reward of right contemplation?
The revelation that it is all
Gravel and moss and rocks and clipped
Shrubbery. That it doesn't
Symbolize anything at all.
The birds are quite aware
Of its meaning. They ignore
Monastery walls and are
Furiously mating everywhere
In the hot perfumed sunlight.
The secret of the moss garden
Is sprinkling it just enough,
Depending on the weather,
And sweeping it twice a day
So lightly the leaves are removed,
And the moss is stimulated.
Except for the ancient masterpiece
That hangs in the kakemono
The best calligraphy in this

Monastery is a white strip
Of plain typing paper, on it
In straightforward clerk's hand:
"These examples of cloud writing
By our saintly Zen Master
Are for sale for fifteen thousand yen each."
I am startled to discover
The Papilio Indra
Has gone as the day grew cool
And the smaller black butterfly
I had thought was still him
Is one of the rarest that flies,
Found only in Kyoto.
Like the owl of Minerva
He is still flying as the sunset
Makes long patches of
Ruddy gold on moss and lichened
Maple trunks and the gongs
Ring for evening prayers
All about us, temple calling
To temple, and the doves in
The eaves murmur sleepily,
And the swallows fly one last
Circuit, and the bats come out
Under the half moon. I walk
Slowly away through the outer
Garden as the sounds of night,
Both of city and forest,
Grow around me. Outside the
Monastery workmen have
Been repairing the wall and
Have left three neat piles of rubbish.
Red earth, white gravel, yellow
Wet clay and straw. A little
Further along is a neat
Stack of cobbles. The ground is
Carefully swept between the
Four mounds and around a pine tree
And a stump cut off at ground
Level. The strokes of the broom
Make interlocked spirals in the dust.

On the other side of the wall
Is the famous garden, a long
Rectangle of white raked gravel
Separated from another
Equal rectangle of moss
With two standing rocks, a spreading
Pine, and some azalea bushes.
The bushes echo the shapes
Of the vast distant mountains.
The sea is placid. The forest
Drowses in the sunset. Far
Away the Himalayas
Guard the world from all trouble.
The hands move from gesture to
Gesture. "Peace to the earth."
"I protect you from evil."
"I am the source of power."
"I turn the orbits of the planets."
"The mind rests in the clear void."

VIII

The dust of man's trouble rises
And makes the sunset's rosy glow.
The full moon appears on the
Horizon above the temple
Of Dainichi as an
Immense, incomprehensible
Silence overwhelming the world,
The orb of wonder, not moving,
But growing like an obsession.
The salvation of Amida
Has enraptured both the monk
And the householder, but the
Prostitute worships in her
Own way all through the white night.
The promise of the vow of
The Bodhisattva is so
Powerful the stormy ocean of

Karma turns to an unruffled mirror.
The guardians of the gates
Of life cannot sleep for the
Cries of the winged bundles
Of consequence that fly from
Life to life, never finding bliss.
Chidori, chidori,
The looms and pachinko balls
Echo each other and the nightjar
Cries in the incense scented
Garden as the moon shadows move.
The rising of the real moon brings
No light, its setting no darkness.
Ecstasy is luxury.
The crystal mirror of man's affairs
Hangs in the star thinned heaven,
Transparent; nothing is reflected
In it. Only the ghosts of
Grasping, the imaginary
Permanent residents, are
Visible, a rabbit pounding
Bitter herbs, a toad, and a ˉ
Dancing virgin, an exiled thief.
Where is the three legged crow?
He is flying across the
Solar system to the moon—
The mascot of Dainichi.
My heart is not a mirror.
I cannot see myself in it.
If thee does not turn to the
Inner Light, where will thee turn?
Night deepens. In the corner of
The ceiling a black centipede
With fiery red feet lurks by the
Web of a terrified spider.
I rise from my book and fetch
A broom and save the spider.
Altair and Vega climb heaven.
Across the Milky Way the Eagle
Plays the Lyre with his rays.

IX

Under the full moon strange birds
Call in the ancient cedars
Behind the high temple walls.
Or perhaps they are tree toads,
Or the high clear notes come from
The clappers of watchmen monks.
They converse all the warm night.
Toak. tolk. tock. toak. toik. tok. tok.
The bamboos are like plumes of
Incense in the dim moonlight.
The branches of the cedars
Are like great black clouds. The moon
Travels from one to another
As we walk slowly under them.
Owls come and go without sound.
If the full moon is the symbol
Of Amida, who is the half moon?
The half moon is the embrace
Of Shaka and Tara.
Midnight.
The clatter of the looms
Is louder than when other
People are working. They are
Weaving a kimono with
Colors like the fluctuant
Ocean and an obi of
Flowers amongst rocks at the
Edge of the snow on a summer
Mountain. The owls stop flying
And cry from garden to garden.
A huge red moth flies around
The lantern. The butterflies
Sleep. So do the swallows.
So do the pigeons. So even
Do the bats. The air is sweet
With the scents of a May night,
And the faint smell of incense
At each temple gate. A bell.

And then gongs sound from every
Compound, and temple by temple,
The chanting of the monks.
The looms go on as they have always done.
   Click clack click click clack click
Cho Cho
   Click clack click click clack click
Cho Cho.

X

The sound of gongs, the songs of birds,
The chanting of men, floating wisps
Of incense, drifting pine smoke,
Perfume of the death of Spring—
The warm breeze clouds the mirror
With the pollen of the pines,
And thrums the strings of the lute.
Higher in the mountains the
Wild cherry is still blooming.
The driving mist tears away
And scatters the last petals,
And tears the human heart. Altair
and Vega climb to the zenith.
A long whistling wail on the flute,
The drummer makes a strangling cry.
And to the clacking of the sticks,
The weaving girl dances for
Her cowboy far across the
Cloudy River. Wings waver
And break. Pine boughs sigh in the
Dark. The water of life runs
Quick through dry reeds.
Under the full moon, a piercing
Fragrance spreads through the white night
Like the perfume of new snow.
An unknown tree has blossomed
Outside my cabin window.

In the warm night cold air drains
Down the mountain stream and fills
The summer valley with the
Incense of early Spring. I
Remember a grass hut on
A rainy night, dreaming of
The past, and my tears starting
At the cry of a mountain cuckoo.
Her bracelets tinkle, her anklets
Clink. She sways at her clattering
Loom. She hurries to have a new
Obi ready when he comes—
On the seventh day of the seventh
Month when the pachinko balls
Fall like meteor swarms.
   Click clack click click clack click
Cho Cho
   Click clack click click clack click
Cho Cho
   Toak. tolk. tock. toak. toik. tok. tok.
Chidori. Chidori.
Kannon. Kannon.
The great hawk went down the river
In the twilight. The belling owl
Went up the river in the
Moonlight. He returns to
Penelope, the wanderer
Of many devices, to
The final woman who weaves,
And unweaves, and weaves again.
In the moon drenched night the floating
Bridge of dreams breaks off. The clouds
Banked against the mountain peak
Dissipate in the clear sky.

A SONG AT THE WINEPRESSES

for Gary Snyder

It is the end of the grape
Harvest. How amiable
Thy dwellings, the little huts
Of branches in the vineyards
Where the grape pickers rested.
Adieu, paniers, vendanges sont faites.
Five months have passed. Here am I—
Another monastery
Garden, another waterfall,
And another religion,
Perched on the mountain's shoulder,
Looking out over fogbound
Santa Barbara. Cactus
And stone make up the garden,
At its heart a heavy cross.
Off behind the monastery,
Deep in the canyon, a cascade
Of living water, green and white,
Breaks the arid cliffs, twisting
Through yellow sandstone boulders,
Sycamores, canyon oaks, laurels,
Toyonberries, maples, pines.
Buzzards dream on the wing, high
On the rising morning air.
A canyon wren sings on a dead
Yucca stem. Over a high rock
Across the stream, a bobcat
Peeks at me for a moment.
A panting doe comes down to drink.
And then the same water ouzel
I just saw above Kyoto.
Passing through the dry valley
Of gum trees, they make it a place
Of springs, and the pools are filled
With water. Deep calls to deep
In the voice of the cataracts.

Loving kindness watches over
Me in the daytime and a song
Guards me all through the starlit night.
Altair and Vega are at
The zenith in the evening.
The cowboy has gone back
Across the Cloudy River.
The weaving girl is pregnant
With another year. The magpie
Wing bridge of dreams has dissolved.
The new wine dreams in the vat.
Low over the drowsy sea,
The sea goat moves towards the sun.
Richard of St. Victor says,
"Contemplation is a power
That coordinates the vast
Variety of perception
Into one all embracing
Insight, fixed in wonder on
Divine things—admiration,
Awe, joy, gratitude—singular,
Insuperable, but at rest."
The sparrow has found her a home,
The swallow a nest for herself,
Where she may raise her brood.
When we have tea in the loggia,
Rusty brown California towhees
Pick up crumbs around our feet.
The towhees were pets of the Indians.
They are still to be found on
The sites of old rancherias,
Waiting for the children to
Come and feed them acorn cakes.
Just so the swallows still nest
In the eaves of all the buildings
On the site of the vanished
Temple in Jerusalem.
Above us from the rafters
Of the loggia hang two wooden
Mexican angels; on their rumps

Are birds' nests. The Autumn sun
Is a shield of gold in heaven.
The hills wait for the early rain
To clothe them in blessings of flowers.
It is the feast of Raphael
The archangel, and Tobit
And the faithful dog.

Mt. Calvary, Santa Barbara, 1967

THE SPARK IN THE TINDER
OF KNOWING

for James Laughlin

Profound stillness in the greystone
Romanesque chapel, the rush
Of wheels beyond the door only
Underlines the silence. The wheels
Of life turn ceaselessly.
Their hiss and clank is
The noiseless turning of the Wheel
Of the Law, that turns without
Moving, from zenith to nadir,
From plus to minus, from black to white.
Love turns the uncountable,
Interlocking wheels of the stars.
The earth turns. The sun sets.
A bolt of iron all on fire
Falls into the turning city.
Love turns the heart to an unknown
Substance, fire of its fire.
Not by flesh, but by love, man
Comes into the world, lost in
The illimitable ocean
Of which there is no shore.
The sea of circumstance where
The heart drowns is the sea of love.

The heart drinks it and it drinks
The heart—transubstantiation
In which the One drinks the Other
And the Other drinks the One.
The sea of fire that lights all being
Becomes the human heart.
No place. No place.
Moon. Sun. Stars. Planets.
Water. Rivers. Lakes. Ocean.
Fish in them. The swimming air.
Birds and their flying.
All turn to jewels of fire,
And then to one burning jewel.
The feathered heart flies upward
Out of this universe.
The broken heart loses its plumes
And hides in the earth until
It can learn to swim in the sea.
Empty the heart and peace will fill it.
Peace will raise it until it floats
Into the empyrean.
It is love that produces
Peace amongst men and calm
On the sea. The winds stop. Repose
And sleep come even in pain.
Peace and windlessness and great
Silence arise in midheaven.
That which appears as extant
Does not really exist,
So high above is that which truly is—
Reality enclosed in the heart,
I and not I, the One
In the Other, the Other
In the One, the Holy Wedding.
Innumerable are the arrows
In love's quiver and their flight
Defines my being, the ballistics
Of my person in time.

Cowley Fathers, Cambridge, 1968

Complete descriptive catalog available free on request from
New Directions, 333 Sixth Avenue, New York 10014.   † Bilingual